SCHOLASTIC

Teaching Resources for the *System 44* Library

Secondary

Credits appear on page 112, which constitutes an extension of this copyright page.

Copyright © 2009 by Scholastic Inc.

All rights reserved   Published by Scholastic Inc.   Printed in the U.S.A.

ISBN-13: 978-0-545-07834-4
ISBN-10: 0-545-07834-2

SCHOLASTIC, SYSTEM 44, SCHOLASTIC READING COUNTS!, SCHOLASTIC READING INVENTORY, READ 180, and associated logos and designs are trademarks and/or registered trademarks of Scholastic Inc. LEXILE and LEXILE FRAMEWORK are registered trademarks of MetaMetrics, Inc. Other company names, brand names, and product names are the property and/or trademarks of their respective owners.

1 2 3 4 5 6 7 8 9 10   10   17 16 15 14 13 12 11 10 09 08

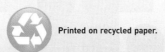

Printed on recycled paper.

Table of Contents

Conference Guides and Wrap-Ups

Additional Resources

Introduction to the *System 44* Library

The *System 44* Library is a collection of 36 high-interest, age-appropriate texts for struggling readers. The Library provides opportunities for students who are developing decoding skills to apply their skills to motivating, relevant texts that use the language and features of authentic fiction and nonfiction texts. The books promote practice and review of essential phonics concepts in text that is controlled for difficulty. The purpose of the *System 44* Library is to:

- engage students with high-interest, age-appropriate fiction and nonfiction texts that promote successful independent reading practice and reading enjoyment.

- practice phonics skills and build on students' expanding knowledge of sound-spelling correspondences and high-frequency words.

- build fluency through independent practice, repeated reading, and teacher instruction.

- build vocabulary through repeated exposure to content-specific and general academic vocabulary words.

- build endurance with increasingly longer and more challenging text.

- develop listening comprehension through use of audiobooks.

Library Components

System 44 Library

The 36 books in the *System 44* Library cover diverse genres and topics. These books have been analyzed using the Lexile Framework®—a highly accurate system that matches students to materials at their level so they can read with success.

These books provide opportunities for students to review and practice decoding and fluency skills introduced on the *System 44* Software and in the *Teaching Guide.* Important phonics and word study elements—called Phonics Focus—are listed on the inside back cover of each book and on the Library Overview on **pages 10–15** of this guide.

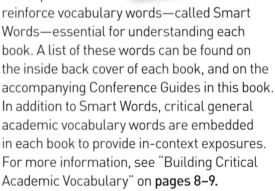

Additionally, the books present and reinforce vocabulary words—called Smart Words—essential for understanding each book. A list of these words can be found on the inside back cover of each book, and on the accompanying Conference Guides in this book. In addition to Smart Words, critical general academic vocabulary words are embedded in each book to provide in-context exposures. For more information, see "Building Critical Academic Vocabulary" on **pages 8–9.**

The *System 44* Library books gradually increase in difficulty, as shown in the chart below.

	Books 1–16	Books 17–28	Books 29–36
Software Connection	Series 1–10	Series 11–18	Series 19–25
Lexile®	100–250	200–350	300–450
Page Count	8–16 pp.	16–24 pp.	24–32 pp.
Smart Words	3–5	6	7
Art	Art on every page	Art on approximately every 3 pages	Art on approximately every 4 pages

Teaching Resources for the *System 44* Library

This book is organized into the following sections:

- **Using the *System 44* Library in the Classroom** This section provides instructions for using the Conference Guides, Wrap-Ups, and Routines in the classroom.

- **red** **Building Critical Academic Vocabulary** This article presents background and practical information for developing academic vocabulary through independent reading.

- **Library Overview** This chart provides at-a-glance information regarding Library titles, genres, Phonics Focus, Smart Words (including Spanish cognates), and general academic vocabulary words.

- **red** **Routines** Teaching routines may be used with the Conference Guides to help reinforce decoding skills, vocabulary-building strategies, and fluency skills.

- **Conference Guides** Teaching resources for each Library title present book summaries and resources for conferencing and reinforcing decoding, vocabulary, fluency, and comprehension skills.

- **Wrap-Ups** These reproducible practice pages, also available through the Scholastic Achievement Manager (SAM), provide students with comprehension and writing activities to promote accountable reading.

- **Graphic Organizers** The reproducible Word Sort, Vocabulary Builder, and Fluency Checklist provide additional support for building decoding skills, vocabulary, and fluency.

- **Reading Log** This reproducible graphic organizer allows students to track their reading progress.

- **Answer Key** Answers are provided for the activities Wrap-Up pages.

System 44 Audiobooks

Recordings of each book may be used to scaffold student access to the text and to promote listening comprehension. The audiobooks present two voices:

- **The Reading Coach,** who introduces the book, previews the book's Smart Words and Phonics Focus, and prompts students to react to the story.

- **The Narrator,** who reads aloud, modeling fluent reading of the text.

System 44 Reading Counts! Quizzes

Scholastic Reading Counts! quizzes provide computer-based multiple-choice questions for each *System 44* Library book. These quizzes help you monitor successful book completion. (See the *Assessment and Reporting Guide* for additional information.)

Using the *System 44* Library in the Classroom

The phonic elements targeted in the *System 44* Library are based on a scope and sequence that gradually increases in difficulty. You may wish to have students read the books in order, assign books based on Lexile (use SAM reports to access students' Lexile scores), or have students choose books based on their own preferences. The following is recommended procedure for using these books:

1 **Preview** Begin by previewing the book. Read the title and back cover information. Point out the Phonics Focus words and Smart Words listed on the inside back cover. Tell students that the Phonics Focus words present examples of sounds, patterns, or word parts they will encounter often as they read the book. Explain that the Smart Words are vocabulary words they will encounter as they read the book. Preview Smart Word definitions (given at the beginning of the book) with students, or have students listen to the audiobook to hear a recorded introduction to the Smart Words.

2 **Discuss and Monitor** Have students read the book independently, with a partner, or with your support as needed. Recordings of each book may be used to scaffold student access to the text and build listening comprehension. During and after reading, use the book summary and comprehension questions in the Conference Guide to engage students in discussion and to monitor comprehension. To foster accountable reading and provide comprehension and writing practice, have students complete the Wrap-Up activity provided for each book.

3 **Instruct** Use the resources provided in the Conference Guides to assess students' need for instruction in decoding, vocabulary building, and fluency related to their reading. Follow the directions in the Conference box for each instructional option. In cases where there is a need for further instruction, proceed to the Individualized Instruction box.

4 **Reinforce** Use the Routines provided on **pages 16–29** in this book to remediate and reinforce skills.

5 **Record** Guide students to use the Vocabulary Builder on **page 103**, Fluency Checklist on **page 104**, and Reading Log on **page 105** to record their progress.

6 **Assess and Track Progress** Use *Scholastic Reading Counts!* electronic quizzes to assess book completion and generate progress reports.

System 44 Library Conference Guides

Conference with students to build skills, promote accountability, and guide reading response.

- **Phonics Focus**
  Indicates the Phonics Focus of the book.

- **Book Summary**
  Gives a brief book synopsis for teacher reference.

- **Wrap-Up**
  Provides student materials for comprehension and writing practice that may be photocopied or printed from SAM and distributed to students.

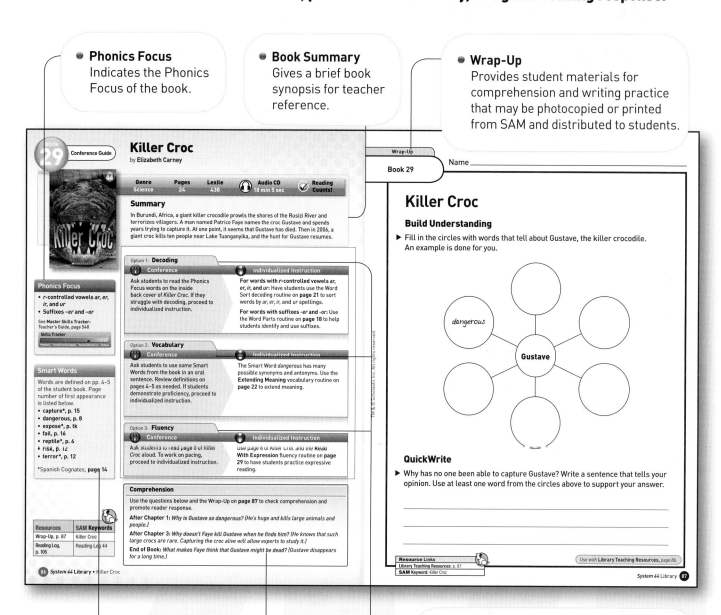

- **Smart Words**
  Lists the Smart Words that are highlighted and explained in the book.

- **Comprehension Questions**
  Offers engaging questions to promote oral discussion of the book and monitor comprehension.

- **Instructional Options**
  Provides a plan for quickly surveying students' grasp of decoding skills and vocabulary associated with the book, as well as their reading fluency. For each instructional option, assess the need for instruction by following the directions in the Conference box. Progress to Individualized Instruction as needed.

Vocabulary Development

- The average student learns 2,000 to 3,000 words each year, mostly by reading words in context.
- Instruction for struggling readers should help students learn morphologically connected academic words through repeated in-context encounters.

Students need frequent opportunities for independent reading of texts that contain critical general academic words in context.

Dr. Elfrieda H. Hiebert

Building Critical Academic Vocabulary

What Is Academic Vocabulary?

In the middle grades, students are faced with textbooks that present a vast increase in the amount and complexity of academic vocabulary. This is when students with vocabulary problems begin to struggle (RAND Reading Study Group, 2002).

There are different types of academic vocabulary. One type, technical vocabulary, includes subject-specific words. Usually these words are introduced to students as the focus of content-area instruction (Graves, 2000), so that students will learn terms like *democracy* and *oligarchy* in the social studies classroom and terms like *photosynthesis* and *cytoplasm* in the science classroom as these concepts are being introduced.

Another category of academic vocabulary, sub-technical or general academic vocabulary (Coxhead, 2000), consists of more general words such as *consider*, *system*, *form*, and *structure* that appear across multiple subjects. General academic words vary in meaning in different contexts and act as different parts of speech. For example, a science text may describe the *form* that matter takes, while a social studies text may describe the way in which a government was *formed*.

While general academic words are just as crucial to academic success as technical vocabulary, they are not often deliberately taught. In addition, since they appear infrequently in nonacademic texts, students are less likely to learn these words outside of the classroom.

The Critical Academic Word List (CAWL)

Many of the general academic vocabulary words incorporated throughout the *System 44* Library come from the Critical Academic Word List (Hiebert, 2008). Unlike other lists of general academic words that were developed for university students learning English as a second language (Coxhead, 2000), the Critical Academic Word List (CAWL) was specifically designed to include the general academic words most critical to the academic success of elementary- and middle-school students.

Determining Which Words Make the List

To compile the CAWL, researchers used the following criteria:

1. **Frequency** The list contains words predicted to appear with at least moderate frequency in elementary- and middle-grade texts, particularly content-area texts.

2 **Morphological Richness** According to Carlisle and Katz (2006), words that appear with some frequency increase the likelihood of recognition of other members of their morphological family. While the word *visualize* is rare, *visual, vision, visible,* and *invisible* occur with moderate frequency in written texts. The CAWL, therefore, includes less commonly occurring words that are part of semantically linked morphological families. This inclusion enables teachers to direct students' attention to similarities and differences between the meanings of words within each family.

3 **Dispersion** This term refers to the degree to which words appear across different subject areas. A word such as *form* appears across many subject areas, while a word such as *adverb* appears mostly in the context of language arts. The CAWL contains words dispersed widely across different subject areas.

The CAWL in Practice: Word Learning Strategies

Research indicates that the average student learns from 2,000 to 3,000 words each year, and that most of this learning is done by reading words in context, not through approaches that attempt to teach words one at a time (Anderson & Nagy, 1992).

Students need frequent opportunities for independent reading of texts that contain critical words in context. The books in the *System 44* Library provide students with repeated exposures to words from the CAWL. Each book contains a list of Smart Words that includes selected general academic vocabulary words from the CAWL as well as content-specific vocabulary words that are essential for book comprehension. Additionally, scaffolded vocabulary support is presented at the back of each book and in this guide.

Differentiating Instruction

✓ **Reinforcing Book Vocabulary** Guide students to review the Smart Words and their definitions provided in each book, and use the audiobooks to build meta-cognitive awareness of these words. Discuss word meaning and have students use words in sentences.

✓ **Morphological Word Families** Foster students' word consciousness by associating Smart Words with related words. Use the Extending Meaning vocabulary routine on **page 22** to guide students to make connections among words.

✓ **Vocabulary Building Practice** Teach strategies to help students unlock word meaning through word analysis and context clues. See the Multiple-Meaning Words Routine on **page 23** and the Context Clues Routine on **page 24**.

✓ **Independent Application** Encourage students to use the Vocabulary Builder graphic organizer on **page 103** to record and learn new words they encounter during reading.

References

- Anderson, R., & Nagy, W. (1992). "The Vocabulary Conundrum." *American Educator* (16)4, 14–18.
- Carlisle, J.F. & Katz, L. A. (2006). "Effects of Word and Morpheme Familiarity on Reading of Derived Words." *Reading and Writing, 19,* 669–693.
- Coxhead, A. (2000). "A New Academic Word List." *TESOL Quarterly,* 34(2), 213–238.
- Graves, M. F. (2000). "A Vocabulary Program to Complement and Bolster a Middle-Grade Comprehension Program." *Reading for Meaning: Fostering Comprehension in the Middle Grades.* Teachers College Press.
- Hiebert E.H. (2008). "Identifying a Critical Form of Vocabulary in Middle-Grade, Content-Area Texts." [Online] Available: http://www.textproject.org
- RAND Reading Study Group (2002). "Reading for Understanding: Toward a Research and Development Program in Reading Comprehension." Washington, DC: RAND.

Library Overview Lexile range 100–250

This chart provides an overview of the Lexile, genre, Phonics Focus, and vocabulary coverage of each book. Vocabulary coverage includes:

- **Smart Words:** Words essential for understanding each book that students should attend to before, during, and after reading.
- **General Academic Words:** Critical general academic words embedded in each book to provide in-context exposures. For more information on general academic words, see "Building Critical Academic Vocabulary" on **pages 8-9**.

Title	Genre	Phonics Focus	Smart Words (With Spanish Cognates)	General Academic Words
1 Bugs That Kill LEXILE 200	science	✔ Short vowels *a, e, i, o, u* (an, at, big, bug, can, get, has, if, in, mad, mob, mantis, nab, not, odd, run, tip, web, yum) ✔ Consonants *b, d, g, p* (big, bug, get, mad, mob, nab, tip, web)	poison spider sting	body
2 Messy Jobs LEXILE 150	jobs	✔ Short vowels (bags, big, bin, bits, can, cuts, dig, fixes, fun, gets, has, hits, job, lots, man, mixes, rocks, rots, in, is, it, wins) ✔ –s and –es endings (bits, cuts, digs, dips, fixes, gets, lots, mixes, rocks, rots, wins)	machine *(máquina)* stink waste	machine
3 Yes! LEXILE 200	social studies	✔ s- blends (scans, skid, skin, slam, slip, snag, snaps, spills, spin, spots, step, sticks, stop, stuff, stuns) ✔ Double consonants (chill, huffs, mess, miss, puffs, spills, stuff, will, yells)	achieve compete *(competir)* score	achieve, compete
4 Fast! The World's Fastest Couch and Other Fast Things LEXILE 150	science	✔ Blends (blast, brisk, desk, fast, glad, grip, must, plan, plant, rest, risk, sprigs, strap, trip, twigs, twins)	limit *(límite)* rate vehicle *(vehículo)*	rate, reach, travel
5 These Are Not Poems LEXILE 210	poetry	✔ Review blends (bring, skull, smells, stick) ✔ -ng and -nk (bring, hunk, junk, rank, sings, sink) ✔ Double consonants (confess, express, mess, miss, skull, smells, tell, well, will)	confess *(confesar)* express *(expresar)* hero *(héroe)*	express, practice, true
6 Wonders of the World LEXILE 240	social studies	✔ Blends (act, gift, help, lift, plants, ramp, send, sent, stand, went)	build statue *(estatua)* wonder	act, attacks, moved, united
7 What's New? A History of Invention LEXILE 230	science	✔ Closed syllables (actress, biggest, cannot, gimmick, happens, helmet, invent, plastic, problem, products)	date design *(diseñar)* event *(evento)* invent *(inventar)* science *(ciencia)*	invent, invents, invented, invention, inventions, move, order, science, separate

Title	Genre	Phonics Focus	Smart Words (With Spanish Cognates)	General Academic Words
8 **Yo, Yolanda! Advice About Friends** LEXILE 130	life issues	✔ Digraph *sh* (bash, blush, cash, clash, crush, fresh, gushes, rush, shed, shift, shock, shot, trash, wish)	advice assume forgive mistake problem *(problema)*	advice, assume, borrows, family, mean, moved, moving, need, nervous, usually
9 **Is This Art?** LEXILE 230	social studies	✔ *ch* and *–tch* (attach, batch, bunch, catch, chat, chip, check, chill, chump, chunks, drenches, lunch, French, match, much, stretches, such)	artist *(artista)* change create *(crear)* familiar *(familiar)* sculpture *(escultura)*	disagree, created, creates, dangerous, familiar, simple
10 **DJ Mystery** LEXILE 190	fiction	✔ *th* (math, path, Seth, thank, Thadd, that, them, then, thin, thing, think, this, with)	crowd excite *(excitar)* invite *(invitar)* record truth	mean, mystery, truth
11 **Survival Guide: How to Keep Your Job** LEXILE 190	jobs	✔ *-ing* with no base change (acting, asking, bringing, brushing, catching, checking, fixing, gossiping, happening, listing, messing, picking, punishing, snatching, spilling, sticking, telling, thinking, willing, yelling) ✔ Review *ch, -tch, sh, th* (brushing, catch, chat, checking, chicken, hush, much, punishing, sandwich, shop, snatching, that, them, then, things, think, this, with)	customer fire focus *(enfocar)* reason *(razón)* responsible *(responsable)*	follow, matter, mean, need, nervous, office, raise, reasons, refuse, responsible, rules, sign, supplies, truth
12 **Fashion Flashback** LEXILE 220	social studies	✔ *-ed* ending with no base change (acted, blasted, dressed, ended, expected, fixed, instructed, jazzed, lasted, lifted, limited, matched, missed, packed, shifted, shocked, stacked, stomped, tricked, wished)	decade *(década)* fashion popular *(popular)* practical *(práctico/a)* trend	fashion, history, introduction, popular, rule, simple, trend
13 **Button Your Lip and Other Idioms** LEXILE 210	language arts	✔ Closed syllables with *schwa* (button, common, finish, gossip, happens, jacket, kitchen, kitten, piglets, problem)	common *(común)* explain *(explicar)* idiom shake tale	explain, explains, mean, means, need, person, true
14 **African Journey** LEXILE 230	science	✔ Consonants + *-al, -el,* or *-le* (animals, cattle, jungle, little, mammals, middle, rental, simple, single, travel)	local *(local)* migrate *(migrar)* national *(nacional)* nature *(naturaleza)* travel	attack, circle, energy, group, guide, labeled, national, photos, raise, travel
15 **Ripped From the Headlines** LEXILE 210	social studies	✔ Long *a* and *i* with final *e* (alive, blaze, brave, came, crime, fine, fire, five, grade, grave, hike, hikes, inside, lane, life, made, pipe, plane, plate, ride, rides, safe, save, side, tales, time, waves, wide) ✔ Long *i* with final *e* (crime, fine, fire, five, hike, inside, life, pipe, ride, side, time, wide)	amaze believe brave danger rescue *(rescatar)*	act, acted, aid, amaze, amazed, choice, energy, formed, move, normal, protect, survive, true
16 **The Princess Brat** LEXILE 220	fiction	✔ Soft *c* and *g* (budge, cage, cell, chance, face, gentle, judge, nice, Princess, rage, spice, twice) ✔ Suffix *-ment* (contentment, excitement)	agreement famous *(famoso/a)* raise reality *(realidad)* stomp	agreement, gentle, meant, need, relax, simple

Library Overview Lexile range 200–350

Title	Genre	Phonics Focus	Smart Words (With Spanish Cognates)	General Academic Words
17 **Cool Jobs in Basketball** LEXILE 300	jobs	✔ Words with VCe (advice, athlete, came, collide, combine, compete, desires, dispute, drove, games, grades, hired, hires, hope, huge, inside, Jones, made, name, notes, promote, relate, shape, site, spoke, whole, woke, write) ✔ Prefixes *non-* and *un-* (nonathletes, nonstop, unexpected, unpacks)	**athlete** *(atleta)* **business** **experience** *(experiencia)* **hire** **intern** *(interno/a)* **rely**	able, advice, appear, base, became, combine, combined, confides, decisions, desires, encouraged, exercises, experience, realized, relate, special
18 **When Lisa Met Billy** LEXILE 220	graphic novel/fiction	✔ *–ing* with base change (budding, challenging, chatting, dating, exciting, getting, kidding, liking, quitting, saving, stopping, trembling) ✔ Review *–ing* with no base change (acting, happening, helping, picking, shocking, telling)	**director** *(directoro/a)* **nervous** *(nervioso/a)* **quit** **realize** **rehearse** **role** *(rol)*	agreed, amazing, challenging, choice, course, director, exciting, family, mean, meant, need, nervous, realize, response, truth, understand
19 **Crash!** LEXILE 320	science	✔ *–ed* with no base change (crushed, filled, happened) ✔ *–ed* with base change (died, excited, exploded, named, placed, raced, sized, slammed, spotted, tugged) ✔ *y* as a vowel (by, fly, gravity, sky, study, system)	**expert** *(experto/a)* **follow** **gravity** *(gravedad)* **orbit** *(órbita)* **telescope** *(telescopio)*	damaged, experts, follow, form, formed, move, need, powerful, ready, reasons, scientists, simple, system, universe
20 **Back From the Grave!** LEXILE 240	classic retelling	✔ Suffixes *–y* and *–ly* (closely, lucky, quickly, sadly) ✔ Change y to i (angrily, cried, tried)	**bury** **coffin** **dream** **examine** *(examinar)* **remove** **worry**	agreed, became, body, course, decided, examined, expecting, identify, possibly, raised, servant, treated
21 **El Tiburón** LEXILE 340	social studies	✔ Silent letters *wr-* and *-mb* (numb, wrapped, wreck) ✔ *ph* (phone) ✔ Digraph *wh-* (when, whip, why) ✔ Review endings *-ed , -ing* (asking, completed, crashing, decided, ended, escaped, flipped, getting, helping, hired, jumped, lifted, popping, standing, stopping, swimming, tried, trying, using, waiting, wrapped, yelled)	**accident** *(accidente)* **attempt** **complete** *(completar)* **hope** **purpose** *(propósito— this is closer to "goal"; fin is closer to "reason")* **support**	attempt, became, choose, currents, dangerous, decided, disabled, means, moved, purpose, reached, reason, separates, supported
22 **Medical Miracle** LEXILE 340	science	✔ Open syllables (baby, even, fatal, final, finally, human, located, open, table, vital) ✔ Unstressed open syllables (adults, capital, confident, medical)	**artery** *(arteria)* **fused** *(fusionado/a)* **prepare** *(preparar)* **stretch** **surgery** *(cirugía)* **syndrome** *(síndrome)*	body, confident, confused, located, need, needed, operate, operates, operating, operation, prepare, prepared, ready, signs, true

Title	Genre	Phonics Focus	Smart Words (With Spanish Cognates)	General Academic Words
23 **Disaster!** LEXILE 330	science	✔ *com-* and *con-* (combined, common, completely, computed, concrete, construct, contacted, contributed, convinced)	aid damage escape *(escapar)* massive *(masivo)* survivor warning	aid, compared, damage, damaged, decided, deliver, destroyed, determined, family, followed, form, formed, level, natural, needed, power, reached, survive, united, warning
24 **The Sweater Thief** LEXILE 250	fiction	✔ Long *a* vowel teams (afraid, away, chain, complain, contained, day, explain, faint, gray, Kayla, main, okay, paid, pay, remain, say, stay, wait, way)	confused *(confundido/a)* employee *(empleado/a)* expensive ignore *(ignorar)* include *(incluir)* praise	acting, confused, contained, counter, course, definitely, employee, entrance, experience, explain, group, ignored, instant, raise, receipt, remain, true, truth, usually
25 **Left to Die** LEXILE 350	science	✔ Long *o* vowel teams *oa* and *ow* (approached, below, blowing, boast, crowed, floating, followed, goal, groaned, grow, know, known, load, moaned, road, show, slow, snow, stow, tow)	approach gear glacier *(glaciar)* struggle summit vertical *(vertical)*	amazing, approached, approaching, base, became, choice, dangerous, determined, difficult, excitement, followed, matter, needed, reached, reason, struggled, survive, survived, view
26 **Samurai Fighters** LEXILE 300	social studies	✔ Long *e* vowel teams *ea, ee,* and *ie* (beat, defeat, disagree, each, easy, free, greedy, keep, means, need, piece, pleaded, read, see, sneak, teaches, team, thieves, three, weak)	clan *(clan)* defeat emperor *(emperador)* enemy *(enemigo/a)* legend *(leyenda)* samurai *(samurai)*	became, defeat, disagree, enemies, enemy, expert, former, less, loyal, mean, means, need, needed, power, powerful, practice, prepares, respect, respected, rule, ruled, serve, served, sign, special, true
27 **Ant Attack!** LEXILE 290	classic retelling	✔ Prefixes *pre-* and *re-* (prejudge, refill, relight, return) ✔ Long *i igh* (fight, frightened, light, might, night, relight, right, sight, tightly) ✔ Other long *i* spellings (behind, find, kind, wild) ✔ Long *o* spellings (bold, bolted, jolted, told)	attack *(atacar)* drown horror *(horror)* invade *(invadir)* precaution *(precaución)* reassure	approached, attack, became, body, moving, raised, reached, survive, survived, unable, warned
28 **Witch Hunt** LEXILE 300	social studies	✔ Multiple affixes (bewitched, unlucky) ✔ Ending *-ed* with base change (accused, begged, believed, blamed, changed, cried, disliked, hired, lied, named, released, tried) ✔ Suffixes *–ly* and *–y* (crazy, lucky, quickly, really, strangely, unlucky)	accuse *(acusar)* admit *(admitir)* hearing release rumor *(rumor)* trial	acting, admit, admitted, choices, decide, figure, governor, increase, needed, release, respected, special, strict, truth, unusual

LEXILE RANGE 200–350

Library Overview Lexile range 300–450

Title	Genre	Phonics Focus	Smart Words (With Spanish Cognates)	General Academic Words
29 **Killer Croc** LEXILE 430	science	✔ *r*-controlled vowels *ar, er, ir,* and *ur* (better, car, expert, far, first, hard, large, monster, November, number, return, river, scars, smart, survivors) ✔ Suffixes *-er* and *-or* (hunters, killer, ranger, survivors, swimmers)	capture *(capturar)* dangerous expose *(exponer)* fail reptile *(reptil)* risk terror *(terror)*	attacked, attacking, attacks, body, capture, captured, choice, collects, dangerous, decided, disappeared, disappears, enter, entered, excited, expert, experts, figured, follow, includes, less, move, moved, need, needed, photograph, polluted, possible, ranger, respect, scientist, sense, sign, truth, view
30 **The Promise** LEXILE 440	social studies	✔ *r*-controlled vowels *or* and *ore* (before, born, forced, forms, more, north, northern, orphan, orphanage, reform, reported, story, torn, Victoria) ✔ */sh/* spellings *ci* and *ti* (direction, inspiration, nation, physician, vacation, vicious)	accomplish activist *(activista)* conflict *(conflicto)* continue *(continuar)* dedicate *(dedicar)* mission *(misión)* reform *(reformar)*	able, accomplish, action, actions, affects, agree, aids, attacked, attacks, avoid, became, body, choose, conflict, connection, continue, continued, continues, dangerous, decision, direction, divided, educated, encourages, enemies, enemy, equipment, family, formed, government, group, moved, nation, need, needed, patient, patients, prevent, protects, raised, rates, reason, reported, reporter, resistance, signs, survive, system, tension, treat
31 **Beauty and the Geek** LEXILE 380	fiction	✔ *r*-controlled vowels *-air, -are,* and *-ear* (care, compare, fair, hair, pair, rare, scared, shared, unfair, upstairs, wears) ✔ Suffixes *-er* and *-est* (biggest, cuter, fastest, finest, happier, happiest, harder, hardest, later, nicer, nicest, older)	compare *(comparar)* impress *(impresionar)* interest *(interés)* introduce *(introducir)* jealous obvious *(obvio)* plan *(plan)*	admit, choice, collection, compare, confused, convinced, course, excited, expected, impress, impressed, introduced, mean, needed, nervous, perfect, perfectly, practice, truth
32 **Fire! The Triangle Shirtwaist Factory Tragedy** LEXILE 440	social studies	✔ Diphthongs *oi, oy, ou,* and *ow* (about, avoid, choice, crowded, down, enjoy, ground, joined, now, oil, out, powered, powerful, powerless, shout) ✔ Suffixes *-ful* and *-less* (careful, careless, fearless, hopeful, powerful, powerless, tireless, useless)	factory *(factoría—more commonly "fábrica")* improve labor *(labor—used in the sense of "task" rather than a larger concept of "work")* prevent *(prevenir)* protest *(protestar)* strike tragic *(trágico)*	act, agreed, became, charged, choice, created, danger, dangers, decision, enjoy, family, follow, focus, government, groups, important, improve, investigate, investigating, means, members, moved, movement, moving, need, needed, offices, powered, powerful, powerless, prevent, prevented, protect, protected, protection, reached, ready, refused, remind, respond, responded, rules, support, survive, treated, warn

Title	Genre	Phonics Focus	Smart Words (With Spanish Cognates)	General Academic Words
33 **Hot Jobs** LEXILE 450	jobs	✔ Variant vowel /oo/ and /ew/ (balloon, Baloo, blew, classroom, cool, crew, flew, food, foolish, grew, knew, loomed, moonlight, new, oozing, room, school, shoot, soon, too, tools, zoom) ✔ Prefixes *mid-* and *sub-* (midday, midnight, midsummer, submerged) ✔ Roots *dict* and *port* (important, predict, report, transports)	career *(carrera)* equipment *(equipo)* extreme *(extremo)* handle major *(mayor—means both "of great importance" and "older")* result *(resultado)* train	act, action, aid, become, challenging, communication, current, danger, dangerous, enjoy, equipment, expert, experts, extreme, flows, graduated, important, less, major, mean, means, meant, nature, need, needed, object, observatory, offered, office, possible, practice, protect, resists, result, scientist, special, subjects, survive, warning
34 **Everyday Heroes** LEXILE 440	social studies	✔ *oo* and *u* (book, Brooklyn, foot, good, hook, looked, misunderstood, onlookers, pull, pushing, put, shook, stood, took, wool) ✔ Prefixes *dis-* and *mis-* (disable, discover, discovery, misunderstood) ✔ Roots *rupt, struct,* and *scrib/script* (abruptly, construction, describe, instructed, instructions, interrupted, script)	discovery distract *(distraer)* distress hesitate instruct *(instruir)* maneuver *(maniobra)* station *(estación)*	able, act, acting, action, appeared, approached, arrived, attack, attacked, balance, body, certain, charge, collection, construction, counter, crime, curve, danger, decided, discover, discovery, discussed, disturbing, enjoyed, family, followed, gently, ignored, instructions, less, location, matter, mattered, meant, memorial, move, moving, need, needed, nervous, nervousness, noticed, occurred, offered, perform, protect, reached, recalling, received, serving, signs, struggled, survive, united, unusual
35 **Arabian Nights** LEXILE 340	graphic novel/ classic retelling	✔ *a, au,* and *aw* (all, awful, called, caused, dawned, fraud, haunted, launch, law, outlaw, saw, small, straw) ✔ Suffixes *-sion* and *-tion* (action, condition, decision, invasion, location) ✔ Root *graph* (graphic)	advisor betray greedy majesty *(majestad)* nightmare supply treasure	accept, acted, action, advisor, agreed, allow, appeared, arrived, attack, become, body, certain, character, course, decision, disappeared, enemy, entered, entering, family, followed, instantly, located, location, mean, need, offered, person, powerful, powers, raised, reach, ready, realized, recognize, servant, special, supply, trade, traded, warning
36 **Lost! Mysteries of the Bermuda Triangle** LEXILE 440	science	✔ Prefix *tri-* (triangle) ✔ Suffixes *-able* and *–ible* (believable, drinkable, favorable, impassable, inescapable, reasonable, responsible, sensible, unavoidable, unbearable, unexplainable, unfavorable, unforgettable, unpredictable, unsinkable, usable) ✔ Roots *phon, scope, tele,* and *vis/vid* (telephones, telescopes, televisions, visible, visited)	current *(corriente)* disappear *(desaparecer)* panic *(pánico)* surrounded unpredictable *(impredicible)* violent *(violento/a)* visible *(visible)*	attack, attacked, attacks, avoid, base, connect, course, current, currents, danger, dangerous, destroy, destroyed, direction, disappear, disappeared, enter, existed, experts, explain, explains, explanation, explanations, explored, favorable, form, information, located, mean, mysterious, mystery, need, predict, predicting, reasonable, reasons, report, reports, responsible, scientists, sense, signs, surrounded, transport, type, united, usually, violent, visible, warning

Why Use Decoding Routines?

- These routines help students match sounds with the symbols used to represent them in words.
- Orally blending words helps students decode words while reading.
- Decoding skills lead to rapid word recognition, greater fluency, and improved comprehension.
- As students develop decoding skills, they become more able to devote their full attention to making meaning from text.

Purpose

Recognizing syllable patterns helps students correctly determine vowel sounds and decode unfamiliar words.

Decoding Routines

Use these brief and playful routines with books in the System 44 *Library to help students grasp sound-symbol relationships.*

Use these routines to provide fast-paced support. To maximize benefits to students be sure to:

- Repeat tasks as often as necessary until students demonstrate success.
- Modify tasks to help students who demonstrate difficulty.
- Informally monitor students during decoding routines and select those who need additional intervention.
- Provide additional support as needed by backtracking to an easier step or providing more cues and examples.

Syllable Strategies

Guide students to read and write multisyllabic words with open and closed syllables.

1 Have students write the Phonics Focus words from the book on a piece of paper. Review key syllable concepts, including:

- Every syllable has just one vowel sound.
- Syllables that end in a consonant are called closed syllables and usually have a short vowel sound.
- Syllables that end in a vowel are called open syllables and usually have a long vowel sound.

2 Guide students to use the Look, Spot, Split, and Read strategy to analyze and read the words. This strategy is available in the *44Book*, page 184, for students' reference.

Look for any prefixes, suffixes, or endings you know.
- Remember, the spelling of the base word may have changed when the ending or suffix was added.

Spot the vowels in the base word. The number of vowel spots tells the number of syllables.
- Remember, some vowel sounds are spelled with more than one letter.

Split the word into syllables.
- A good place to split a word is between two consonants.
- If there is only one consonant between syllables, try splitting after it.

Read the word. Does it make a real word? If not, you may need to split the word in a different place or try using a different vowel sound.

Syllable Type Examples

Book	Syllable Type	Phonics Focus Words
Book 7: *What's New? A History of Invention*	Closed Syllables	actress, biggest, cannot, gimmick, happens, helmet, invent, plastic, problem, products
Book 13: *Button Your Lip and Other Idioms*	Closed Syllables with Schwa	button, common, finish, gossip, happens, jacket, kitchen, kitten, piglets, problem
Book 14: *African Journey*	Consonant + *-al*, *-el*, or *-le*	animals, cattle, jungle, little, mammals, middle, rental, simple, single, travel
Book 22: *Medical Miracle*	Open Syllables	baby, even, fatal, final, finally, human, located, open, table, vital
	Unstressed Open Syllables	adults, capital, confident, medical

Blends and Digraphs

Guide students to recognize common consonant blends and digraphs.

1 Write a list of words on the board or on a piece of paper, some with consonant blends and some with consonant digraphs, and have students copy the words. Try to pick a sampling of words that shows blends and digraphs in the beginning, middle, and end positions. (Check the charts below for possible examples.)

2 Explain that a consonant blend is two or more consonants that appear together in a word, with each retaining its own sound. Point out an example from the list of words.

3 Explain that a consonant digraph is two consonants that stand for one sound, such as *ch*, *sh*, and *th*. Point out an example from the list of words.

4 Ask students to read each word on the list, circle the consonant blends, and underline the digraphs.

Purpose

Recognition of digraphs and familiarity with common consonant blends lead to improved decoding and automaticity.

Blends Examples

Book	Phonics Focus Words
Book 3: *Yes!*	scans, skid, skin, slam, slip, snag, snaps, spills, spin, spots, step, sticks, stop, stuff, stuns
Book 4: *Fast! The World's Fastest Couch and Other Fast Things*	blast, brisk, desk, fast, glad, grip, must, plan, plant, rest, risk, sprigs, strap, trip, twigs, twins
Book 5: *These Are Not Poems*	bring, hunk, junk, rank, sink, skull, smells, stick
Book 6: *Wonders of the World*	act, gift, help, lift, plants, ramp, send, sent, stand, went

Digraphs Examples

Book	Phonics Focus Words
Book 5: *These Are Not Poems (and Other Poems)*	bring, sings
Book 8: *Yo, Yolanda! Advice About Friends*	bash, blush, cash, clash, crush, fresh, gushes, rush, shed, shift, shock, shot, trash, wish
Book 9: *Is This Art?*	attach, batch, bunch, catch, chat, chip, check, chill, chump, chunks, drenches, lunch, French, match, much, stretches, such
Book 10: *DJ Mystery*	math, path, Seth, thank, Thadd, that, them, then, thin, thing, think, this, with
Book 11: *Survival Guide: How to Keep Your Job*	brushing, catch, chat, checking, chicken, hush, much, punishing, sandwich, shop, snatching, that, them, then, things, think, this, with
Book 21: *El Tiburón*	when, whip, why

Word Parts

Students identify and define prefixes, suffixes, inflectional endings, and roots.

Prefixes

1. Review with students that a prefix is a word part that can be added to the beginning of a base word to change its meaning. *For example, the prefix* mis- *means "wrong." The word* misunderstood *means that someone has understood wrongly or incorrectly.*

2. Ask students to list Phonics Focus words with prefixes. Then, ask them to write out the prefix and base word as an addition problem for each word. For example, the word *misunderstood* would be written as follows: *mis- + understood = misunderstood.*

3. Ask students to read each word part separately and then put the parts together to read the whole word.

Prefixes Examples

Book	Prefix	Phonics Focus Words
Book 17: *Cool Jobs in Basketball*	non- un-	nonathletes, nonstop, unexpected, unpacks
Book 23: *Disaster!*	com- con-	combined, common, completely, computed, concrete, construct, contacted, contributed, convinced
Book 27: *Ant Attack!*	pre- re-	prejudge, refill, relight, return
Book 28: *Witch Hunt*	be- un-	bewitched, unlucky
Book 33: *Hot Jobs*	mid- sub-	midday, midnight, midsummer, submerged
Book 34: *Everyday Heroes*	dis- mis-	disable, discover, discovery, misunderstood
Book 36: *Lost! Mysteries of the Bermuda Triangle*	tri-	triangle

Suffixes and Inflectional Endings

1 Explain that suffixes are word parts that can be added to the end of a base word to change the word's meaning or part of speech. *For example, the suffix* -ful *means "full of." The word* hopeful *means "full of hope." Adding* -ful *to the noun* hope *creates the adjective* hopeful. Explain that inflectional endings may make a noun plural, change the tense of a verb, or help a verb agree with its subject.

2 Ask students to list words with suffixes or endings from their current book, leaving room to write beneath each word. Then, ask them to write out the base word and suffix or ending as a math equation for each word. For example, the word *hopeful* would be written as follows: *hope + -ful = hopeful*.

Note: Remind students that adding suffixes or endings to some base words requires spelling changes. Help them include these changes in their equations (for example: *happy – y + i + -ness = happiness; nice – e + -er = nicer; big + g + -est =* biggest). For words with suffixes *-tion, -sion, -able,* and *-ible,* ask students to divide the word into syllables then create an equation by adding the syllables and suffix or ending (for example: *ac + -tion = action; un- + pre- + dict + -able = unpredictable*).

3 Ask students to read each word part separately and then put the parts together to form the whole word.

Suffixes Examples

Book	Suffix	Phonics Focus Words
Book 16: *The Princess Brat*	-ment	contentment, excitement
Book 20: *Back From the Grave!*	-y -ly	closely, lucky, quickly, sadly, angrily
Book 28: *Witch Hunt*	y -ly	crazy, lucky, quickly, really, strangely, unlucky
Book 29: *Killer Croc*	-er -or	hunters, killer, ranger, survivors, swimmers
Book 31: *Beauty and the Geek*	-er -est	biggest, cuter, fastest, finest, happier, happiest, harder, hardest, later, nicer, nicest, older
Book 32: *Fire! The Triangle Shirtwaist Factory Tragedy*	-ful -less	careful, careless, fearless, hopeful, powerful, powerless, tireless, useless
Book 35: *Arabian Nights*	-sion -tion	action, condition, decision, invasion, location
Book 36: *Lost! Mysteries of the Bermuda Triangle*	-able -ible	believable, drinkable, favorable, impassable, inescapable, reasonable, responsible, sensible, unavoidable, unbearable, unexplainable, unfavorable, unforgettable, unpredictable, unsinkable, usable

RULES TO KNOW: Suffixes and Endings

Rule 1

VC + ending that begins with a vowel = double the final consonant

EXPLANATION: When a word ends with a short vowel followed by a single consonant, double the final consonant before adding a suffix or ending that begins with a vowel *(hopped, running, muddy)*.

Rule 2

silent *e* + ending that begins with a vowel = drop the silent *e*

EXPLANATION: When a word ends with a silent *e*, drop the *e* before adding a suffix or ending that starts with a vowel *(racing, finer)*.

Rule 3

consonant-*y* + ending that begins with a vowel = change *y* to *i* (except *-ing*)

EXPLANATION: When a word ends with a consonant and *y*, change the *y* to *i* before adding a suffix or ending that starts with a vowel, except for *-ing* *(dutiful, luckily, muddier, dried, babies, crying)*.

ADDITIONAL ROOTS FOR INSTRUCTION

Greek Roots

hydro (water)

meter (measure)

ology (word or study)

photo (light)

therm (heat)

EXAMPLES

hydrogen, hydroplane
thermometer, perimeter
geology, zoology
photography, photocopy
thermos

Latin Roots

aud (to hear)

ject (to throw)

tract (to draw or pull)

EXAMPLES

audience, audio
reject, inject, eject
tractor, attract, extract

Anglo-Saxon Roots

kno (skill)

lik (similar, to be pleased with)

tru (faithful)

EXAMPLES

know, knowledge, knew
like, likeness, likely
truth, true, truly

Inflectional Endings Examples

Book	Inflectional Ending	Phonics Focus Words
Book 2: *Messy Jobs*	-s -es	bits, cuts, digs, dips, fixes, gets, lots, mixes, rocks, rots, wins
Book 11: *Survival Guide: How to Keep Your Job*	-ing with no base change	acting, asking, bringing, brushing, catching, checking, fixing, gossiping, happening, listing, messing, picking, punishing, snatching, spilling, sticking, telling, thinking, willing, yelling
Book 12: *Fashion Flashback*	-ed with no base change	acted, blasted, dressed, ended, expected, fixed, instructed, jazzed, lasted, lifted, limited, matched, missed, packed, shifted, shocked, stacked, stomped, tricked, wished
Book 18: *When Lisa Met Billy*	-ing with base change	budding, challenging, chatting, dating, exciting, getting, kidding, liking, quitting, saving, stopping, trembling
	-ing with no base change	acting, happening, helping, picking, shocking, telling
Book 19: *Crash!*	-ed with no base change	crushed, filled, happened
	-ed with base change	died, excited, exploded, named, placed, raced, sized, slammed, spotted, tugged
Book 20: *Back From the Grave!*	-ed with base change	cried, tried
Book 21: *El Tiburón*	-ed and -ing	asking, completed, crashing, decided, ended, escaped, flipped, getting, helping, hired, jumped, lifted, popping, standing, stopping, swimming, tried, trying, using, waiting, wrapped, yelled
Book 28: *Witch Hunt*	-ed with no base change	bewitched
	-ed with base change	accused, begged, believed, blamed, changed, cried, disliked, hired, lied, named, released, tried

Roots

Remind students that many words in the English language come from Greek, Latin, and Anglo-Saxon roots. *Knowing the meanings of roots can help you figure out the meanings of words you don't know. For example, the root* tele *means "far off," and the root* scope *means "to see." A telescope lets you see things that are far away.*

Ask students to list words with roots from their current book. Then, ask them to circle all of the roots they can find in each word. Guide students to explain how the root of each word contributes to the word's meaning. Students should use dictionaries as needed.

Roots Examples

Book	Root Words	Phonics Focus Words
Book 33: *Hot Jobs*	*dict, port*	important, predict, report, transports
Book 34: *Everyday Heroes*	*rupt, struct, scrib/script*	abruptly, construction, describe, instructed, instructions, interrupted, script
Book 35: *Arabian Nights*	*graph*	graphic
Book 36: *Lost! Mysteries of the Bermuda Triangle*	*phon, scope, tele, vis/vid*	telephones, telescopes, televisions, visible, visited

Word Sort

Guide students to practice putting familiar words into groups according to their sounds and/or spellings.

This routine can be used with most Phonics Focus elements. The example below uses Phonics Focus words with *r*-controlled vowels from Book 29, *Killer Croc*.

Have students use the Word Sort graphic organizer on **page 102** to sort the Phonics Focus words *better, car, expert, far, first, hard, large, monster, November, number, return, river, scars, smart,* and *survivors* into groups according to their vowel spellings: *ar, ir, er, ur, or.*

Ask students to identify a pattern or principle that is operating and state it aloud. For example, students may conclude that there are three ways to spell the /ûr/ sound as seen in the words *experts, return,* and *first.*

Purpose

Word sorting enhances visual and auditory attention to the internal details of words and helps students remember correct spellings for words with vowel sounds that can be spelled more than one way.

This routine works with a variety of Phonics Focus elements.

Why Use Vocabulary/Word Study Routines?

- These routines give students tools they can use to understand and build vocabulary as they read.
- Vocabulary is fundamental to comprehension. Students cannot understand text without knowing what most of the words mean.
- Having a wide vocabulary is beneficial in building comprehension, as well as overall academic success.

Purpose

Students who practice reading words from different morphological families are more likely to notice familiar base words in longer words.

Associating words with synonyms and antonyms helps students build a larger vocabulary and develop reasoning skills.

Vocabulary/Word Study Routines

Use these routines to help your students build vocabulary.

These routines will equip students with strategies for unlocking unfamiliar words and building vocabulary as they read.

Extending Meaning

Guide students to look for connections among words with the same base, root, or meaning.

Morphological Word Families

Have students write an appropriate Smart Word on a piece of paper. Guide students to notice if the word is formed from a base word, or whether it is a base word itself. Work together to create a list of other words with the same base. For example, the following words share the base *present*: *represent*, *presentation*, *misrepresent*, and *presentable*. Discuss how the base word relates to the meaning of each word.

For words with familiar Greek or Latin roots, ask students to come up with words they know that use the root. For example, the word *telescope* includes the root *tele*, meaning "far off." This root is shared with the words *television*, *telephone*, and *telegraph*. Discuss how the root contributes to the meaning of each word.

Discuss how identifying a familiar word part or base can help students figure out the meaning of an unfamiliar word as they read.

Examples

Book	Smart Word	Word Family
Book 5: *These Are Not Poems (and Other Poems)*	express	expressed, expresses, expressing, expression, expressions, expressive, unexpressive
Book 7: *What's New? A History of Invention*	invent	inventing, invented, inventions, inventor, inventive
Book 13: *Button Your Lip and Other Idioms*	explain	explained, unexplained, explaining, explains, explainable, unexplainable, explanation, explanatory
Book 16: *The Princess Brat*	agreement	agree, agreeable, agreeing, agreements, disagree, disagreement
Book 21: *El Tiburón*	support	supporters, supportive, supporting
Book 24: *The Sweater Thief*	employee	employ, employed, employees, employer, employers, employing, employment, employs
Book 30: *The Promise*	activist	act, action, active, activate, activity, actor, actress
Book 34: *Everyday Heroes*	discovery	discover, discovered, discoveries, discovering, discovers
Book 35: *Arabian Nights*	advisor	advice, advised, advises, advisors, advising, advisory, advisable, unadvisable

Synonyms and Antonyms

Have students write an appropriate Smart Word on a piece of paper. Challenge students to make a list of as many synonyms (words with similar meanings) and antonyms (words with opposite meanings) as they can think of, with the aid of a thesaurus if necessary.

Examples

Book	Smart Word	Possible Synonyms	Possible Antonyms
Book 2: *Messy Jobs*	messy	dirty, untidy, filthy, grimy, cluttered, sloppy	clean, tidy, neat
Book 17: *Cool Jobs in Basketball*	rely	trust, have faith in, depend on, count on	distrust, doubt, question
Book 18: *When Lisa Met Billy*	quit	cease, end, give up, leave, stop, resign	start, continue, pursue, stick with
Book 20: *Back From the Grave!*	remove	subtract, take away, delete	add, remain, keep
Book 23: *Disaster!*	aid	help, assist, relieve, support, back	hurt, block, harm, injure
Book 29: *Killer Croc*	dangerous	risky, unsafe, hazardous, perilous, threatening	safe, harmless, secure, protected

Multiple-Meaning Words

Guide students to learn to use context to help determine the correct meaning for multiple-meaning words.

1 **Define Multiple-Meaning Words** Tell students that some words have more than one meaning. To figure out a word's meaning, readers must use clues from the sentence or surrounding sentences.

2 **Identify Multiple-Meaning Words** Introduce students to a multiple-meaning word, and provide at least two alternate meanings. Present the word in context by reading the sentence or sentences in which it appears, and then think aloud to demonstrate how you determine which meaning best fits the context.

This example uses the multiple-meaning word *hearing* from page 13 of Book 28, *Witch Hunt*:

Read the second paragraph aloud. Tell students that the word *hearing* has multiple meanings. *Hearing* can mean "perceiving sound," or "a meeting in a court of law to hear the facts about a case." *The sentences tell about women taken to a courtroom to be asked questions by a judge. These clues help me see that the right meaning for hearing is "a meeting in a court of law to hear the facts about a case."*

3 **Practice** Ask students to use each meaning of the multiple-meaning word in a written sentence.

Purpose

Knowledge of multiple-meaning words helps students develop strategies for identifying correct word meaning, to build text comprehension.

Examples of Smart Words with Multiple Meanings

Book	Page and Paragraph	Smart Word	Meanings
Book 1: *Bugs That Kill*	Page 5, paragraph 2	sting	"to bite or stick with something sharp" or "a wound or pain"
Book 2: *Messy Jobs*	Page 3, paragraph 3	waste	"to throw something away before it's used" or "garbage"
Book 6: *Wonders of the World*	Page 3, paragraph 1	wonder	"something that's amazing or surprising" or "to be curious about something"
Book 9: *Is This Art?*	Page 4, paragraph 2	change	"to make something different" or "money in the form of coins"
Book 10: *DJ Mystery*	Page 11, paragraph 4	crowd	"a large group of people" or "to not give someone enough room"
Book 15: *Ripped From the Headlines*	Page 4, paragraph 1	brave	"not afraid" or "to do something unpleasant and difficult," as in "He braved the storm."
Book 19: *Crash!*	Page 7, bottom paragraph	follow	"to watch or keep track of something" or "to chase or pursue"
Book 28: *Witch Hunt*	Page 13, paragraph 2	hearing	"perceiving sound" or "a court trial"
Book 33: *Hot Jobs*	Page 13, paragraph 3	handle	"to deal with or take control" or "the part of an object used to move it"

Context Clues

Students learn strategies to determine the meaning of unfamiliar words based on their context.

1 **Define Context Clues** Explain that when they come across an unfamiliar word, students can sometimes figure out its meaning by looking for clues from other words or sentences around it.

2 **Identify Context Clues** Introduce a Smart Word students are unfamiliar with. Then, read the sentence or paragraph (as needed) in which it appears. Ask students to listen for words that may shed light on the meaning of the unknown Smart Word. Model how to use context clues by thinking aloud for students.

This example uses the Smart Word *strike* from page 14 of Book 32, *Fire! The Triangle Shirtwaist Factory Tragedy*:

I'll read the last paragraph aloud. As I read, I will look for context clues to figure out the meaning of strike. Explain that the sentences "Workers all over New York went on strike. They refused to go back to work until things improved" suggest that a *strike* has to do with workers not working because of problems at their jobs.

Explain that using context clues does not always lead to determining a word's correct meaning. Students need to reread to confirm their ideas. If students find a definition does not fit the context, they should try again or consult a dictionary.

Purpose

Using context clues helps students determine the meanings of unfamiliar words in context, increasing their comprehension and confidence.

3 **Practice** Ask students to use the Vocabulary Builder on **page 103** to jot down unfamiliar words they encounter as they read. First, have them use context clues to figure out the meaning. Next, have them look up the word in the dictionary and compare the definitions. Finally, have them record the dictionary definition.

Examples of Context Clues

Book	Page and Paragraph	Smart Word	Context Clues
Book 11: *Survival Guide: How to Keep Your Job*	Page 12, paragraph 2	focus	You are thinking about friends and music. You need to focus on your job.
Book 14: *African Journey*	Page 8, paragraph 2	migrate	Some animals migrate.... Wildebeests travel really far.
Book 22: *Medical Miracle*	Page 9, paragraph 2	artery	An artery carries a lot of blood.
Book 25: *Left to Die*	Page 6, paragraph 2	vertical	The mountain's West Face is almost vertical. It goes straight up and down.
Book 26: *Samurai Fighters*	Page 12, paragraph 2	legend	One samurai woman became a legend... People said she could not be defeated.
Book 27: *Ant Attack!*	Page 9, paragraph 1	precaution	"The ants will not get us," he assured them. "But we must take precautions!"
Book 32: *Fire! The Triangle Shirtwaist Factory Tragedy*	Page 14, paragraph 4	strike	Workers all over New York went on strike. They refused to go back to work until things improved.
Book 36: *Lost! Mysteries of the Bermuda Triangle*	Page 17, paragraph 2	current	It's like an invisible river in the ocean.

Idioms

Students learn to identify and understand the meaning of idioms.

1 **Define Idioms** Tell students that an *idiom* is a phrase or expression that has a meaning that is different from the literal or actual meaning of the words.

2 **Identify Idioms** Ask students to listen as you read a passage aloud. Identify the idiom and explain its meaning, pointing out how the literal meaning of the words is different from the meaning of the expression. The following example uses the idiom *show off* from page 9 of Book 12, *Fashion Flashback*:

I'll read the second paragraph aloud. As I read, listen for the idiom "show off." Explain to students that *show off* is an idiom that means "to do something to attract attention."

3 **Practice** Have students use the idiom in a few oral sentences.

Purpose

This routine is particularly helpful for students who are new to English, as they may not be familiar with the idiomatic meaning of an expression.

Student Objectives

- Read aloud fluently, with appropriate tone, phrasing, pacing, and expression.

Fluency Routines

Fluency helps students focus on the purpose of reading—extracting and constructing meaning.

Fluency in the Classroom

Timothy Rasinski, a fluency expert and professor of education, defines fluency as "the ability to read quickly, effortlessly, and efficiently with good, meaningful expression." These routines promote fluency by providing practice exercises to support correct phrasing, speed, and expression.

To create meaningful contexts and authentic purposes for fluency instruction and practice, make fluency routines a familiar and regular part of instruction. Give students daily opportunities to read aloud and to gain confidence. Help students see connections between fluent oral and fluent silent reading, and guide them in using fluency terms such as *expression, tone of voice,* and *phrasing*. Use fluency routines with suggested passages from books in the *System 44* Library, or choose your own passages. Add your own ideas, combine methods, and discover the routines that work best for you.

Phrasing and Punctuation

Students learn to read fluently by "chunking" text, making appropriate pauses, and varying their tone.

① **Explain Correct Phrasing** Explain that phrases are groups of words, or "chunks" of text, that go together to make meaning. Fluent readers read in meaningful phrases. Point out that reading with good phrasing helps make a text's meaning clear. Briefly discuss the following qualities of phrasing.

- **Pause** Make a slight pause between the parts of a sentence. Stop to take a breath when you see a comma between words. Pause at the end of a sentence.

- **Express the meaning** Stress some words more than others. Raise or lower the tone of your voice. Read some phrases faster or slower. Express excitement when you see an exclamation mark. Read sentences with question marks as questions.

- **Use Phrasing** Consider beginning a new phrase when you see prepositions such as *with, in, to, by, at, on,* and *for,* and transition words such as *then, next, and, but, or,* and *however.*

② **Model Correct Phrasing** Distribute copies of the Fluency Checklist on **page 104**. Ask students to turn to the selected passages in their books and follow along as you read a paragraph. Read the paragraph in meaningful phrases, emphasizing and slightly exaggerating the phrases. Read with expression at a varied rate, and pause for punctuation.

Ask students to name one quality of fluency they heard in your reading. Have them refer to the Fluency Checklist. Return to the text and identify examples of your phrasing, pauses, emphasis, and expression. Make a check on the list for each quality as it is mentioned.

3 **Practice** Have students read through the passage and identify phrasing cues. They should identify punctuation cues, including commas, periods, question marks, and exclamation marks. They should also look for transition words such as *then, next, and, but, or,* and *however* and prepositions such as *with, in, to, by, at, on,* and *for.* Lastly, ask them to choose a few key words that may be important to stress because of meaning.

For partnered reading, ask students to take turns reading the passage while others listen and fill out the Fluency Checklist. Students who listened should then offer constructive feedback about successes and areas for improvement.

For independent practice, have students use a tape recorder to listen to and to evaluate their reading as they reread the passage, experimenting with different pauses, word stresses, and reading speeds. Offer constructive feedback as needed.

Suggested Passages for Practicing Correct Phrasing

Book	Passage
Book 2: *Messy Jobs*	Pages 4–5
Book 12: *Fashion Flashback*	Pages 10–11
Book 14: *African Journey*	Pages 8–11
Book 17: *Cool Jobs in Basketball*	Pages 8–9
Book 28: *Witch Hunt*	Pages 13–15
Book 32: *Fire! The Triangle Shirtwaist Factory Tragedy*	Pages 9–10

Use Natural, Consistent Pace
Students read and reread for skill, pacing, and accuracy.

1 **Explain Pacing** Briefly discuss how practice makes everything easier—from sports to playing an instrument to cooking. *When people train or rehearse, they practice the same moves, steps, or notes over and over again. Reading is also a skill that can be improved through practice.*

Point out that the best way to make reading automatic is to practice reading the same words again and again. Explain to students that they will practice by reading the same passage several times. Each time they reread the passage, they will begin to recognize more words automatically and will be able to read at a more comfortable pace. They will measure this progress by seeing how much of the passage they can read in one minute. Emphasize that the goal is not to race through the passage, but to read it fluently.

Student Objectives
- Read and reread for speed and accuracy.
- Master unfamiliar words in passages.
- Track fluency progress.

2 **Model Correct Pacing** Ask students to turn to the selected passages in their books. Tell students that you will be timing yourself to see how much of the passage you can read in one minute. Give one student a stopwatch and ask him or her to let you know when one minute is up. Explain that you will be reading for accuracy as well as speed. Ask students to follow along in their books as you read. They should notice where you are at the end of one minute, and make note of any words you read incorrectly.

Read the passage at a natural pace. Read a few simple words incorrectly. Stop reading after a minute, and ask students to identify how many words you misread. Explain that the goal of the exercise is to make sure your pace is not too fast or too slow, and to read all of the words correctly.

3 **Practice** Distribute stopwatches to students. Ask students to read the passage silently several times until they feel comfortable with reading all of the words.

For groups of three, ask students to take turns reading the passage from their books. While one student is reading, the second should be timing the exercise, and the third should be noting errors and the last word read. Students who listened should then offer constructive feedback about successes and areas for improvement.

For independent practice, have students use a tape recorder to record their reading. They should then listen with a stopwatch and make note of errors and the last word read. Periodically check up on their readings and offer constructive feedback as needed.

On subsequent days, provide repeated opportunities to practice the same passage.

Suggested Passages for Practicing Correct Pacing

Book	Passage
Book 4: *Fast! The World's Fastest Couch and Other Fast Things*	Pages 3–5
Book 6: *Wonders of the World*	Pages 3–5
Book 15: *Ripped From the Headlines*	Pages 12–13
Book 22: *Medical Miracle*	Pages 6–8
Book 26: *Samurai Fighters*	Pages 7–9
Book 34: *Everyday Heroes*	Pages 13–15

Read With Expression

Students learn to read in a varied, expressive tone.

1 **Explain Expressive Reading** Ask students to imagine that they are telling a story to their friends. *What are some things you would do to get your friend more interested in the story? Imagine you're telling a scary story. How would you tell it? Imagine you're telling a story about something funny that happened to you. Would you tell that story in the same way you tell a scary story?* Tell students that when they read out loud, it helps to imagine that they are telling a story to a friend and trying to get that friend interested in the story.

Explain that to read with expression, it helps to understand the story. So, before practicing expressive reading, they should read the entire story to understand what is happening in it.

2 **Model Expressive Reading** Ask students to turn to the selected passages in their books and follow along as you read. Read the passage twice. During the first reading, demonstrate how a reader's tone of voice and expression can show different feelings and reflect different characters. Ask students to describe your reading. For the second reading, read the passage flatly, without expression. Ask students to describe the difference.

3 **Practice** Ask students to read the selected text several times until they understand the story and feel comfortable reading all of the words.

For small group practice, distribute copies of the Fluency Checklist on **page 104**. Students should take turns with one reading while others listen and fill out the Fluency Checklist, with special attention paid to the Expression section. Students who listened should then offer constructive feedback about successes and areas for improvement.

For independent practice, have students use a tape recorder to listen to and to evaluate their reading as they reread the same passage, experimenting with varying emotions and emphasis. Offer constructive feedback as needed.

Suggested Passages for Practicing Expressive Reading

Book	Passage
Book 3: *Yes!*	Pages 4–5
Book 13: *Button Your Lip and Other Idioms*	Pages 10–12
Book 19: *Crash!*	Pages 10–11
Book 25: *Left to Die*	Pages 14–15
Book 29: *Killer Croc*	Page 8
Book 35: *Arabian Nights*	Pages 10–12

Purpose

- Rehearse to improve accuracy, phrasing, and prosody.
- Read for comprehension.
- Read to entertain.

BOOK 1

Conference Guide

Bugs That Kill
by **Peggy Bresnick Kendler**

Genre	Pages	Lexile		Audio CD		Reading
Science	8	200		6 min 16 sec		Counts!

Summary

Some bugs must kill to eat or to defend themselves. The tarantula is a big spider that kills bugs and even frogs for food. The praying mantis preys on crickets. Killer bees form a mob when they're angry, and kill by stinging all at once. Scorpions kill by stinging with their poisonous tail. Fire ants have a poisonous bite that burns like fire!

Phonics Focus

- **Short vowels *a, e, i, o, u***
- **Consonants *b, d, g, p***

See **Master Skills Tracker:**
Teacher's Guide, page 548

Skills Tracker

Preteach | Teach/Practice/Apply | Review/Reinforce | Assess

Smart Words

Words are defined on p. 2 of the student book. Page number of first appearance is listed below.

- **poison,** p. 6
- **spider,** p. 3
- **sting,** p. 5

Option 1: **Decoding**

 Conference

Ask students to read the Phonics Focus words on the inside back cover of *Bugs That Kill.* If they struggle with decoding, proceed to individualized instruction.

 Individualized Instruction

For words with short vowels: Have students use the Word Sort decoding routine on **page 21** to sort words by their short vowel sounds.

For words with consonants *b, d, g, p*: Have students use the Word Sort routine to sort words by consonant sounds.

Option 2: **Vocabulary**

 Conference

Ask students to use some Smart Words listed on the inside back cover of *Bugs That Kill* in an oral sentence. Review definitions on page 2 as needed. If students demonstrate proficiency, proceed to individualized instruction.

 Individualized Instruction

The Smart Word *sting* can mean "to bite or stick with something sharp" or "a wound or pain." Use the **Multiple-Meaning Words** vocabulary routine on **page 23** with *sting* as an example to help students use context to determine the correct meaning.

Option 3: **Fluency**

 Conference

Ask students to read page 4 of *Bugs That Kill* aloud. To work on correct phrasing, proceed to individualized instruction.

 Individualized Instruction

Use pages 4–5 of *Bugs That Kill* and the **Phrasing and Punctuation** fluency routine on **page 26** to have students practice correct phrasing.

Comprehension

Use the questions below and the Wrap-Up on **page 31** to check comprehension and promote reader response.

After Page 3: *What does a tarantula eat? (It eats other bugs and even frogs.)*

After Page 4: *What does a praying mantis look like? (It has big eyes and a small head, a green body, and long legs.)*

End of Book: *Why should people avoid killer bees, scorpions, and fire ants? (They can all kill people.)*

Resources	SAM Keywords
Wrap-Up, p. 31	Bugs That Kill
Reading Log, p. 105	Reading Log 44

Name _____

Bugs That Kill

Build Understanding

▶ Details are bits of information. Write two details about each bug. The first one is done for you.

Topic	Details
Tarantula [Page 3]	• This bug is a big spider. • It even eats frogs!
Praying Mantis [Page 4]	
Killer Bee [Page 5]	
Scorpion [Page 6]	
Fire Ant [Page 7]	

QuickWrite

▶ Why do these bugs kill? Explain your answer with details from the book.

_____

_____

_____

Messy Jobs

by **Alan Takamura**

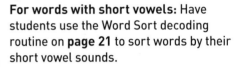

Genre	Pages	Lexile	Audio CD	Reading
Jobs	8	150	7 min 12 sec	Counts!

Summary

Some jobs are messy. Worm farmers dig up worms. Ship painters get covered in paint. Podiatrists handle feet. Clean-up workers mop up oil spills. Motocross bikers race through dirt. Read about the messes people in these jobs face at work.

Phonics Focus

- **Short vowels**
- **-s, -es**

See **Master Skills Tracker:** Teacher's Guide, page 548

Skills Tracker

| Preteach | Teach/Practice/Apply | Review/Reinforce | Assess |

Smart Words

Words are defined on p. 2 of the student book. Page number of first appearance is listed below.

- **machine***, p. 4
- **stink**, p. 3
- **waste**, p. 3

*Spanish Cognates, **page 10**

Option 1: Decoding

Conference

Ask students to read the Phonics Focus words on the inside back cover of *Messy Jobs*. If they struggle with decoding, proceed to individualized instruction.

Individualized Instruction

For words with short vowels: Have students use the Word Sort decoding routine on **page 21** to sort words by their short vowel sounds.

For words with -s and -es: Use the Word Parts decoding routine on **page 18** to help students identify and use inflectional endings.

Option 2: Vocabulary

Conference

Ask students to use some Smart Words listed on the inside back cover of *Messy Jobs* in an oral sentence. Review definitions on page 2 as needed. If students demonstrate proficiency, proceed to individualized instruction.

Individualized Instruction

The Smart Word *waste* can mean "to throw something away before it's used" or "junk or garbage." Use the **Multiple-Meaning Words** vocabulary routine on **page 23** with *waste* as an example to help students use context to determine correct meaning.

Option 3: Fluency

Conference

Ask students to read page 4 of *Messy Jobs* aloud. To work on reading with correct phrasing, proceed to individualized instruction.

Individualized Instruction

Use pages 4–5 of *Messy Jobs* and the **Phrasing and Punctuation** fluency routine on **page 26** to have students practice correct phrasing.

Comprehension

Use the questions below and the Wrap-Up on **page 33** to check comprehension and promote reader response.

After Page 3: *What do farmers do with the worms and droppings? (They sell the worms as fishing bait. They sell the droppings as plant fertilizer.)*

After Page 5: *What is the job of a podiatrist? (A podiatrist's job is to take care of feet.)*

End of Book: *Why is motocross racing a messy job? (It's messy because racers ride in the dirt and get covered in mud.)*

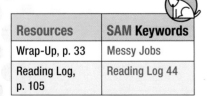

Resources	SAM Keywords
Wrap-Up, p. 33	Messy Jobs
Reading Log, p. 105	Reading Log 44

Name _____

Messy Jobs

Build Understanding

▶ What would each person below say is the messiest part of his or her job? Write what each would say.

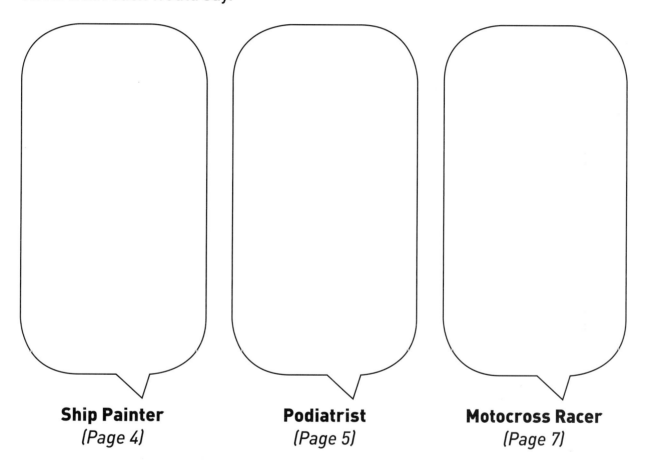

Ship Painter
(Page 4)

Podiatrist
(Page 5)

Motocross Racer
(Page 7)

QuickWrite

▶ Which messy job do you think is the most important? Why? Write a sentence that explains your opinion. Use details from the book to support your answer.

_____

_____

_____

BOOK 3 — Conference Guide

Yes!
by **Ellen Lebrecque**

Genre	Pages	Lexile	Audio CD	Reading
Social Studies	16	200	5 min 47 sec	Counts!

Summary

Sports players have their shining moments. When they do, they shout, "Yes!" From scoring a point to winning a gold medal, victory on the soccer field, ball field, racetrack, or basketball court is sweet.

Phonics Focus

- *s*-blends
- **Double consonants**

See **Master Skills Tracker:**
Teacher's Guide, page 548

Skills Tracker

Preteach | Teach/Practice/Apply | Review/Reinforce | Assess

Smart Words

Words are defined on p. 2 of the student book. Page number of first appearance is listed below.

- **achieve, p. 3**
- **compete,* p. 4**
- **score, p. 3**

*Spanish Cognates, **page 10**

Option 1: Decoding

 Conference

Ask students to read the Phonics Focus words on the inside back cover of *Yes!* If they struggle with decoding, proceed to individualized instruction.

Individualized Instruction

For words with *s*-blends: Use the Blends and Digraphs decoding routine on **page 17** to help students build accuracy.

For words with double consonants: Have students use the Word Sort decoding routine on **page 21** to sort words by their double consonant spellings.

Option 2: Vocabulary

 Conference

Ask students to use some Smart Words listed on the inside back cover of *Yes!* in an oral sentence. Review definitions on page 2 as needed. If students demonstrate proficiency, proceed to individualized instruction.

 Individualized Instruction

The idiom *hot stuff* on page 5 means "someone who is really good at something." Build understanding of idioms using the **Idioms** vocabulary routine on **page 25** with this expression as an example.

Option 3: Fluency

Conference

Ask students to read page 4 of *Yes!* aloud. To work on expressive reading, proceed to individualized instruction.

Individualized Instruction

Use pages 4–5 of *Yes!* and the **Read With Expression** fluency routine on **page 29** to have students practice expressive reading.

Comprehension

Use the questions below and the Wrap-Up on **page 35** to check comprehension and promote reader response.

After Page 4: *What does Shaun White achieve? (the gold medal)*

End of Book: *Why isn't Coach Pete upset when water is dumped on him? (He isn't upset because his team has just won.)*

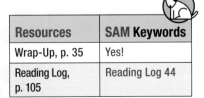

Resources	SAM Keywords
Wrap-Up, p. 35	Yes!
Reading Log, p. 105	Reading Log 44

Yes!

Build Understanding

▶ Explain why each player shouts, "Yes!" An example is done for you.

Shaun White *(Page 4)*

Shaun shouts, "Yes!" because he wins the gold medal.

_____

_____

Chantal Petitclerc *(Page 5)*

_____

_____

Dwight Howard *(Page 6)*

_____

_____

Pete Carroll *(Page 7)*

_____

_____

QuickWrite

▶ Sometimes when players win, they shout "Yes!" Tell about a time when you felt like shouting, "Yes!" Write at least one sentence.

_____

_____

_____

Resource Links
Library Teaching Resources: p. 35
SAM Keyword: Yes!

*Use with **Library Teaching Resources,** page 34.*

System 44 Library **35**

BOOK 4 · Conference Guide

Fast!

by **Juliette Caggiano**

Genre	Pages	Lexile	Audio CD	Reading
Science	**8**	**150**	**5 min 45 sec**	**Counts!**

Summary

Some things are fast—very fast! This book features fast-growing bamboo, high-speed elevators, cheetahs that run 71 miles per hour, a speedy couch you can drive, and space probes that are the fastest vehicles in the sky.

Phonics Focus

• Blends

See **Master Skills Tracker:** Teacher's Guide, page 548

Skills Tracker

Preteach   Teach/Practice/Apply   Review/Reinforce   Assess

Smart Words

Words are defined on p. 2 of the student book. Page number of first appearance is listed below.

• **limit*, p. 5**
• **rate, p. 3**
• **vehicle*, p. 6**

*Spanish Cognates, **page 10**

Option 1: **Decoding**

Conference

Ask students to read the Phonics Focus words on the inside back cover of *Fast!* If they struggle with decoding, proceed to individualized instruction.

Individualized Instruction

For words with blends: Use the Blends and Digraphs decoding routine on **page 17** to help students build accuracy.

Option 2: **Vocabulary**

Conference

Ask students to use some Smart Words listed on the inside back cover of *Fast!* in an oral sentence. Review definitions on page 2 as needed. If students demonstrate proficiency, proceed to individualized instruction.

Individualized Instruction

The idiom *check this out* used in the first paragraph of page 3 means "look at this." Build understanding of idioms using the **Idioms** vocabulary routine on **page 25** with this expression as an example.

Option 3: **Fluency**

Conference

Ask students to read page 3 of *Fast!* aloud. To work on pacing, proceed to individualized instruction.

Individualized Instruction

Use pages 3–5 of *Fast!* and the **Use Natural, Consistent Pace** fluency routine on **page 27** to have students practice reading at a natural pace.

Comprehension

Use the questions below and the Wrap-Up on **page 37** to check comprehension and promote reader response.

After Page 3: *How tall would you be if you grew as fast as bamboo? (miles tall)*

After Page 5: *What are some things that help cheetahs run fast? (Cheetahs have long legs. Their claws grip the ground when they run.)*

End of Book: *What are Helios I and Helios II? (They are space probes, and the fastest vehicles in the sky.)*

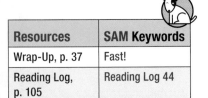

Resources	SAM Keywords
Wrap-Up, p. 37	Fast!
Reading Log, p. 105	Reading Log 44

Name _____

Fast!

Build Understanding

▶ Fill in the circles with words or phrases that tell about the cheetah.
An example is done for you.

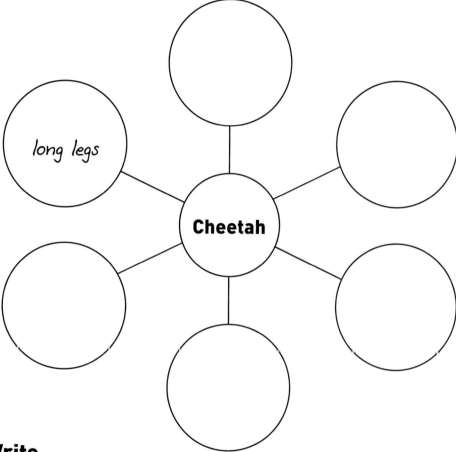

QuickWrite

▶ What other fast object or animal would you add to the book?
Explain what makes your object or animal so fast.

_____

_____

_____

Resource Links
Library Teaching Resources: p. 37
SAM Keyword: Fast!

Use with **Library Teaching Resources,** page 36.

System 44 Library **37**

These Are Not Poems

by **Tina Posner**

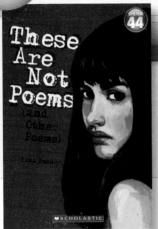

Genre	Pages	Lexile	Audio CD	Reading
Poetry	8	210	6 min 14 sec	Counts!

Summary

This book is as much a journal as a collection of poems, as the introductory poem explains. The four other poems focus on themes such as being more than meets the eye, having a secret crush, learning to be the boss in the kitchen, and living a real life versus a movie life.

Phonics Focus

- **Review blends**
- **Double consonants**
- ***-ng* and *-nk***

See **Master Skills Tracker:** Teacher's Guide, page 548

Skills Tracker

Preteach Teach/Practice/Apply Review/Reinforce Assess

Smart Words

Words are defined on p. 2 of the student book. Page number of first appearance is listed below.

- **confess*, p. 5**
- **express*, p. 3**
- **hero*, p. 7**

*Spanish Cognates, **page 10**

Option 1: Decoding

 Conference

Ask students to read the Phonics Focus words on the inside back cover of *These Are Not Poems*. If they struggle with decoding, proceed to individualized instruction.

 Individualized Instruction

For words with blends, and *-ng* and *-nk*: Use the Blends and Digraphs decoding routine on **page 17** to build accuracy.

For words with double consonants: Have students use the Word Sort routine on **page 21** to sort words by double consonant sounds. Supplement words as needed.

Option 2: Vocabulary

 Conference

Ask students to use some Smart Words listed on the inside back cover of *These Are Not Poems* in an oral sentence. Review definitions on page 2 as needed. If students demonstrate proficiency, proceed to individualized instruction.

 Individualized Instruction

The Smart Word *express* is the base of the words *expressed, expresses, expressing, expression, expressions, expressive,* and *unexpressive*. Use the **Extending Meaning** vocabulary routine on **page 22** to build student familiarity with morphological word families.

Option 3: Fluency

 Conference

Ask students to read page 6 of *These Are Not Poems* aloud. To work on correct phrasing, proceed to individualized instruction.

 Individualized Instruction

Use page 6 of *These Are Not Poems* and the **Phrasing and Punctuation** fluency routine on **page 26** to have students practice correct phrasing.

Comprehension

Use the questions below and the Wrap-Up on **page 39** to check comprehension and promote reader response.

After Page 3: *Why does this poet write poems?* (She writes to express her thoughts and feelings, and to deal with hard times.)

After Page 6: *When is the poet the boss in the kitchen?* (when her mother isn't home)

End of Book: *In what ways is real life different from the movies?* (Movies can make things look easy, but real life is hard work.)

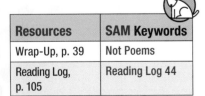

Resources	SAM Keywords
Wrap-Up, p. 39	Not Poems
Reading Log, p. 105	Reading Log 44

Name _____

These Are Not Poems

Build Understanding

▶ The girl writes poems to express her feelings. Write what she might say to answer each question below. The first one is done for you.

Poems are corny.

1. "These Are Not Poems"
What might the reader think about poems?

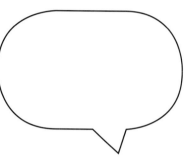

2. "The Me Inside Me"
Who knows the girl best?

3. "My Secret"
What do people love to guess?

4. "The Boss in the Kitchen"
What has the girl learned from her mother?

5. "Real Life"
What do real-life heroes have to do?

QuickWrite

▶ Write a poem about something in your life. Write at least two lines.

_____

_____

_____

BOOK 6 Conference Guide

Wonders of the World
by **Joshua Davis**

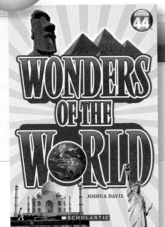

Genre	Pages	Lexile	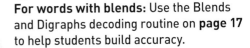 Audio CD	Reading
Social Studies	8	240	6 min 51 sec	Counts!

Summary

The world is full of many wonders. Some, like the Egyptian pyramids, are ancient wonders of the past. Others, like the Internet, are modern-day wonders. This book features seven well-known wonders from near and far.

Phonics Focus

- **Blends**

See **Master Skills Tracker:** Teacher's Guide, page 548

Skills Tracker

Preteach | Teach/Practice/Apply | Review/Reinforce | Assess

Smart Words

Words are defined on p. 2 of the student book. Page number of first appearance is listed below.

- **build, p. 4**
- **statue*, p. 6**
- **wonder, p. 3**

*Spanish Cognates, **page 10**

Option 1: **Decoding**

 Conference

Ask students to read the Phonics Focus words on the inside back cover of *Wonders of the World.* If they struggle with decoding, proceed to individualized instruction.

Individualized Instruction

For words with blends: Use the Blends and Digraphs decoding routine on **page 17** to help students build accuracy.

Option 2: **Vocabulary**

Conference

Ask students to use some Smart Words listed on the inside back cover of *Wonders of the World* in an oral sentence. Review definitions on page 2 as needed. If students demonstrate proficiency, proceed to individualized instruction.

Individualized Instruction

The Smart Word *wonder* can mean "something that is amazing or surprising" or "to be curious about something." Use the **Multiple-Meaning Words** vocabulary routine on **page 23** with *wonder* as an example to help students use context to determine the correct meaning.

Option 3: **Fluency**

 Conference

Ask students to read page 3 of *Wonders of the World* aloud. To work on pacing, proceed to individualized instruction.

Individualized Instruction

Use pages 3–5 of *Wonders of the World* and the **Use Natural, Consistent Pace** fluency routine on **page 27** to have students practice reading at a natural pace.

Comprehension

Use the questions below and the Wrap-Up on **page 41** to check comprehension and promote reader response.

After Page 5: *How many years did it take to build the Great Wall of China? (It took more than 2,000 years.)*

End of Book: *Why did France give the Statue of Liberty to the United States? (France gave it to the United States as a hundred-year birthday present.)*

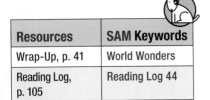

Resources	SAM Keywords
Wrap-Up, p. 41	World Wonders
Reading Log, p. 105	Reading Log 44

Wonders of the World

Build Understanding

▶ Summarize information about each wonder below. Use the most important details from the book. An example is done for you.

Internet *(Page 3)*

The Internet connects people. People use it to find news.

They use it to send emails.

Pyramids of Giza *(Page 4)*

_____

_____

Great Wall of China *(Page 5)*

_____

_____

Statue of Liberty *(Page 7)*

_____

_____

QuickWrite

▶ What is a wonder in your life? Write two sentences to explain why.

_____

_____

What's New? A History of Invention
by Peter Gutiérrez

Genre	Pages	Lexile	Audio CD	Reading
Science	16	230	9 min 58 sec	Counts!

Summary

The time lines in this book show when cool things were invented. These time lines mark scientific milestones in movies, beauty products, sports equipment, transportation, and medicine.

Phonics Focus

- **Closed syllables**

See **Master Skills Tracker:** Teacher's Guide, page 548

Skills Tracker

Preteach | Teach/Practice/Apply | Review/Reinforce | Assess

Smart Words

Words are defined on pp. 2–3 of the student book. Page number of first appearance is listed below.

- date, p. 4
- design*, p. 10
- event*, p. 4
- invent*, p. 5
- science*, p. 8

*Spanish Cognates, **page 10**

Option 1: Decoding

 Conference

Ask students to read the Phonics Focus words on the inside back cover of *What's New?* If they struggle with decoding, proceed to individualized instruction.

Individualized Instruction

For words with closed syllables: Have students use the Syllable Strategies decoding routine on **page 16** to help students determine the correct sound for vowels in closed syllables.

Option 2: Vocabulary

 Conference

Ask students to use some Smart Words from the book in an oral sentence. Review definitions on pages 2–3 as needed. If students demonstrate proficiency, proceed to individualized instruction.

Individualized Instruction

The Smart Word *invent* is the base of the words *inventing, invented, inventions, inventor,* and *inventive.* Use the **Extending Meaning** vocabulary routine on **page 22** with *invention* as an example to build student familiarity with morphological word families.

Option 3: Fluency

 Conference

Ask students to read page 6 of *What's New?* aloud. To work on correct pacing, proceed to individualized instruction.

 Individualized Instruction

Use pages 6–7 of *What's New?* and the **Use Natural, Consistent Pace** fluency routine on **page 27** to have students practice reading at a natural pace.

Comprehension

Use the questions below and the Wrap-Up on **page 43** to check comprehension and promote reader response.

After Page 7: *What is Smell-O-Vision? (an invention that lets people smell movies)*

After Page 9: *Name two inventions on the beauty time line. (Possible answers include: the perm, false eyelashes, tanning lotion, shaving cream, a drug that makes hair grow.)*

End of Book: *Who performed the first open-heart surgery? (Dr. Daniel Hale Williams)*

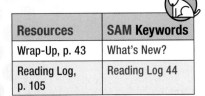

Resources	SAM Keywords
Wrap-Up, p. 43	What's New?
Reading Log, p. 105	Reading Log 44

Name _____

What's New? A History of Invention

Build Understanding

▶ All of the events listed below are from the book, but they are out of order. Rewrite the events in the correct order. The first one is done for you.

Events
Thomas Edison shows movies.
An actress wears false eyelashes.
Doctors test the first fake heart.
A man invents a baseball bat.
Someone invents the first motorcycle.

First
Someone invents the first motorcycle.

⬇

Second

⬇

Next

⬇

Then

⬇

Last

QuickWrite

▶ Which time line is the most interesting? Why? Write a sentence that explains your opinion. Use details from the time line to support your answer.

_____

_____

_____

Resource Links
Library Teaching Resources: p. 43
SAM Keyword: What's New?

Use with **Library Teaching Resources,** *page 42.*

System 44 Library **43**

BOOK 8 | Conference Guide

Yo, Yolanda! Advice About Friends
by **Kim Feltes and Elsa Reyes**

Genre	Pages	Lexile	Audio CD	Reading Counts!
Life Issues	16	130	8 min 21 sec	

Summary

What do you do when friends talk about you behind your back, a pal borrows money but doesn't return it, or a friend has a crush on your brother? How do you make friends at a new school, or make amends for something you did wrong? Teens write to Yolanda looking for help. Yolanda gives advice about dealing with friends.

Phonics Focus

• **Digraph** *sh*

See **Master Skills Tracker:** Teacher's Guide, page 548

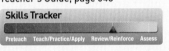

Skills Tracker

Preteach Teach/Practice/Apply Review/Reinforce Assess

Smart Words

Words are defined on pp. 2–3 of the student book. Page number of first appearance is listed below.

• advice, p. 4
• assume, p. 8
• forgive, p. 6
• mistake, p. 4
• problem*, p. 4

*Spanish Cognates, **page 11**

Option 1: Decoding

 Conference

Ask students to read the Phonics Focus words on the inside back cover of *Yo, Yolanda! Advice About Friends*. If they struggle with decoding, proceed to individualized instruction.

 Individualized Instruction

For words with digraph *sh*: Use the Blends and Digraphs decoding routine on **page 17** to help students build accuracy.

Option 2: Vocabulary

 Conference

Ask students to use some Smart Words listed on the inside back cover of *Yo, Yolanda! Advice About Friends* in an oral sentence. Review definitions on pages 2–3 as needed. If students demonstrate proficiency, proceed to individualized instruction.

 Individualized Instruction

The idiom *give them another shot* used in the last paragraph of page 6 means "give them another chance," or "to let them try again." Build understanding of idioms using the **Idioms** vocabulary routine on **page 25** with this expression as an example.

Option 3: Fluency

Conference

Ask students to read page 14 of *Yo, Yolanda! Advice About Friends* aloud. To work on expressive reading, proceed to individualized instruction.

Individualized Instruction

Use page 14 of *Yo, Yolanda!* and the **Read With Expression** fluency routine on **page 29** to have students practice expressive reading.

Comprehension

Use the questions below and the Wrap-Up on **page 45** to check comprehension and promote reader response.

After Page 6: *What does Yolanda say Feeling Trashed should do if her friends say that talking about her was no big deal?* (She advises Feeling Trashed to find new friends.)

After Page 10: *Why is Feeling Used upset at her friend who has a crush on her brother?* (She's upset because her friend comes over all the time, but only wants to see her brother, not her.)

End of Book: *What's Yolanda's advice to the girl who stole her friend's ring?* (Yolanda recommends that she give it back and apologize.)

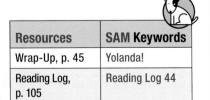

Resources	SAM Keywords
Wrap-Up, p. 45	Yolanda!
Reading Log, p. 105	Reading Log 44

Name _____

Yo, Yolanda! Advice About Friends

Build Understanding

▶ The teens in this book write to Yolanda for advice. Fill in the spaces below with the solution that Yolanda suggests. The first one is done for you.

The Teen's Problem	Yolanda's Solution
1. A girl's friends make fun of her clothes and shoes behind her back. *(Page 6)*	*Yolanda says that the girl should tell her friends that they hurt her feelings.*
2. A boy's best pal keeps borrowing money but doesn't pay him back. *(Page 8)*	
3. A girl doesn't like that her friend wants to come over all the time just to see her brother. *(Page 10)*	
4. A shy girl moves to a new school and needs to make new friends. *(Page 12)*	
5. A girl feels bad about stealing her friend's ring. *(Page 14)*	

QuickWrite

▶ Do you think Yolanda gives good advice? Use at least one solution from above to support your answer.

_____

_____

_____

Resource Links
Library Teaching Resources: p. 45
SAM Keyword: Yolanda!

Use with **Library Teaching Resources,** *page 44.*

System 44 Library 45

Is This Art?

by **Grace Nguyen**

Genre	Pages	Lexile	Audio CD	Reading Counts!
Social Studies	16	230	9 min 46 sec	

Summary

Art can be quite out of the ordinary. Artists create it in all shapes, styles, and sizes—such as a building wrapped in cloth, and a sculpture made from a stool and bicycle wheel. Just what is art and what isn't? That's for every person to decide.

Phonics Focus

- *ch, -tch*

See **Master Skills Tracker:** Teacher's Guide, page 548

Skills Tracker

Preteach Teach/Practice/Apply Review/Reinforce Assess

Smart Words

Words are defined on pp. 2–3 of the student book. Page number of first appearance is listed below.

- artist*, p. 5
- change, p. 4
- create*, p. 6
- familiar*, p. 5
- sculpture*, p. 4

*Spanish Cognates, **page 11**

Option 1: **Decoding**

 Conference

Ask students to read the Phonics Focus words on the inside back cover of *Is This Art?* If they struggle with decoding, proceed to individualized instruction.

Individualized Instruction

For words with *ch* and *-tch*: Use the Blends and Digraphs decoding routine on **page 17** to help students build accuracy.

Option 2: **Vocabulary**

 Conference

Ask students to use some Smart Words listed on the inside back cover of *Is This Art?* in an oral sentence. Review definitions on pages 2–3 as needed. If students demonstrate proficiency, proceed to individualized instruction.

 Individualized Instruction

The Smart Word *change* can mean "to make something be different or new" or "money in the form of coins." Use the **Multiple-Meaning Words** vocabulary routine on **page 23** with *change* as an example to help students use context to determine the correct meaning.

Option 3: **Fluency**

 Conference

Ask students to read page 8 of *Is This Art?* aloud. To work on correct phrasing, proceed to individualized instruction.

 Individualized Instruction

Use pages 8–9 of *Is This Art?* and the **Phrasing and Punctuation** fluency routine on **page 26** to have students practice correct phrasing.

Comprehension

Use the questions below and the Wrap-Up on **page 47** to check comprehension and promote reader response.

After Page 7: *What do artists do for Cow Parade?* (They paint cow sculptures and put them on display.)

After Page 10: *What did Andy Warhol paint pictures of?* (He painted pictures of simple and familiar things.)

End of Book: *Why does Rodney McMillian think that old stuff can be art?* (Old stuff tells an important story about the people who used it.)

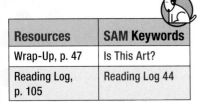

Resources	SAM Keywords
Wrap-Up, p. 47	Is This Art?
Reading Log, p. 105	Reading Log 44

Name _____

Is This Art?

Build Understanding

▶ The artists in this book use all sorts of materials to make their art. Fill in the circles with the names of the different materials or objects they use. An example is done for you.

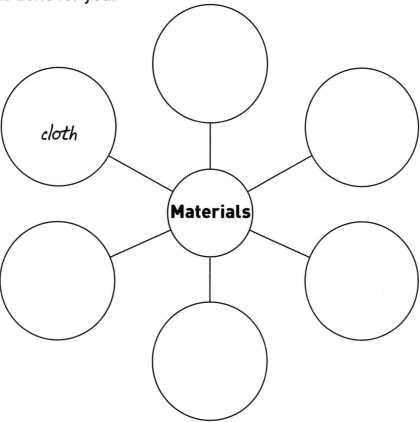

QuickWrite

▶ Do you think that all the works in this book are art? Why or why not? Use some examples from the book to support your answer.

_____

_____

_____

Resource Links
Library Teaching Resources: p. 47
SAM Keyword: Is This Art?

Use with **Library Teaching Resources,** *page 46.*

System 44 Library **47**

DJ Mystery
by **Michael Leviton**

Genre	Pages	Lexile	 Audio CD	Reading
Fiction	16	190	9 min 15 sec	Counts!

Summary

Everyone at Thorn High listens to DJ Mystery's music, but nobody knows that he's really Keith. Seth, the coolest kid at school, wants DJ Mystery to play at his party. Keith decides to go. Everyone is shocked when they learn who the real Keith is. With Seth's help, they learn to see Keith in a whole different light.

Phonics Focus

- *th*

See **Master Skills Tracker:**
Teacher's Guide, page 548

Skills Tracker

Preteach Teach/Practice/Apply Review/Reinforce Assess

Smart Words

Words are defined on pp. 2–3 of the student book. Page number of first appearance is listed below.

- crowd, p. 11
- excite*, p. 4
- invite*, p. 9
- record, p. 4
- truth, p. 5

*Spanish Cognates, **page 11**

Option 1: **Decoding**

Conference

Ask students to read the Phonics Focus words on the inside back cover of *DJ Mystery*. If they struggle with decoding, proceed to individualized instruction.

Individualized Instruction

For words with *th*: Use the Blends and Digraphs decoding routine on **page 17** to help students build accuracy.

Option 2: **Vocabulary**

Conference

Ask students to use some Smart Words listed on the inside back cover of *DJ Mystery* in an oral sentence. Review definitions on pages 2–3 as needed. If students demonstrate proficiency, proceed to individualized instruction.

Individualized Instruction

The Smart Word *crowd* can mean "a large group of people" or "to not give someone enough room." Use the **Multiple-Meaning Words** vocabulary routine on **page 23** with *crowd* as an example to help students use context to determine correct meaning.

Option 3: **Fluency**

Conference

Ask students to read page 6 of *DJ Mystery* aloud. To work on expressive reading, proceed to individualized instruction.

Individualized Instruction

Use pages 6–8 of *DJ Mystery* and the **Read With Expression** fluency routine on **page 29** to have students practice expressive reading.

Comprehension

Use the questions below and the Wrap-Up on **page 49** to check comprehension and promote reader response.

After Page 5: *What do students know about DJ Mystery? (They know he is a fellow student at Thorn High and that he makes cool records.)*

After Page 13: *Why do people have a hard time believing that Keith is DJ Mystery? (They have a hard time believing it because DJ Mystery's music is really cool. Keith, on the other hand, is not popular and some kids call him a loser.)*

End of Book: *What does Seth realize about Keith? (He realizes that no one got to know who Keith really was, and kids judged him unfairly.)*

Resources	SAM **Keywords**
Wrap-Up, p. 49	DJ Mystery
Reading Log, p. 105	Reading Log 44

DJ Mystery

Build Understanding

▶ All of the events listed below are from the book, but they are out of order.
Rewrite each event in the correct order. The first one is done for you.

Events

Jen makes fun of Keith at lunchtime.

Seth invites DJ Mystery to his party.

Seth stops Keith at the door.

Keith dances with Trina.

Trina and Keith talk about going to the party.

Jen asks Keith to dance with her.

First
Seth invites DJ Mystery to his party.

Second

Third

Fourth

Next

Last

QuickWrite

▶ Why do you think Keith chose to dance with Trina instead of Jen?
Explain your answer with details from the book.

_____

_____

_____

BOOK 11 Conference Guide

Survival Guide: How to Keep Your Job
by Chris Kensler

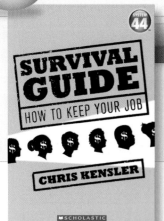

Genre	Pages	Lexile	Audio CD	Reading
Jobs	16	190	10 min 58 sec	Counts!

Summary

People who want to keep their jobs need to know how to deal with problems. What's the best way to deal with a difficult boss? Is it okay to call in sick to have a day off? The advice in this book explains how to deal with these real-life job issues.

Phonics Focus

- *-ing* with no base change
- Review *ch, -tch, sh, th*

See **Master Skills Tracker:** Teacher's Guide, page 548

Skills Tracker

Preteach | Teach/Practice/Apply | Review/Reinforce | Assess

Smart Words

Words are defined on pp. 2–3 of the student book. Page number of first appearance is listed below.

- **customer, p. 9**
- **fire, p. 4**
- **focus*, p. 12**
- **reason*, p. 9**
- **responsible*, p. 7**

*Spanish Cognates, **page 11**

Option 1: Decoding

Conference

Ask students to read the Phonics Focus words on the inside back cover of *Survival Guide.* If they struggle with decoding, proceed to individualized instruction.

Individualized Instruction

For words with *-ing* with no base change: Use the Word Parts decoding routine on **page 18** to help students identify and use inflectional endings.

For words with *ch, -tch, sh,* and *th*: Use the Blends and Digraphs decoding routine on **page 17** to help students build accuracy.

Option 2: Vocabulary

Conference

Ask students to use some Smart Words from the book in an oral sentence. Review definitions on pages 2–3 as needed. If students demonstrate proficiency, proceed to individualized instruction.

Individualized Instruction

Use the **Context Clues** vocabulary routine on **page 24** with the Smart Word *focus* to help students use context clues to determine meaning.

Option 3: Fluency

Conference

Ask students to read page 4 of *Survival Guide* aloud. To work on pacing, proceed to individualized instruction.

Individualized Instruction

Use pages 4–6 of *Survival Guide* and the **Use Natural, Consistent Pace** fluency routine on **page 27** to have students practice reading at a natural pace.

Comprehension

Use the questions below and the Wrap-Up on **page 51** to check comprehension and promote reader response.

After Page 6: *What does the person who works in the deli wonder about? (whether it's okay to take sandwiches and supplies from work)*

After Page 11: *What advice is given about applying for a job you have no experience doing? (Tell the truth. Explain you are willing to learn or be trained.)*

End of Book: *What is wrong with talking to friends or listening to music at work? (These activities are distracting and stop you from concentrating on your job.)*

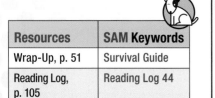

Resources	SAM Keywords
Wrap-Up, p. 51	Survival Guide
Reading Log, p. 105	Reading Log 44

Name ____________________

Survival Guide

Build Understanding

▶ Fill in the chart below with the solution to each problem. An example has been done for you.

Problem	Solution
1. You want to call in sick, but you would be telling a lie. *(Page 7)*	
2. A customer is mean to you every day. *(Page 9)*	Be nice to the customer. This will make your boss happy. It might make the customer happy, too.
3. Your boss is a jerk, and you want to yell at him. *(Page 13)*	
4. You want a raise, but you're too nervous to ask for one. *(Page 15)*	

QuickWrite

▶ Do you agree with every tip in this book? Why or why not? Explain your answer using details from the book.

____

____

____

Resource Links
Library Teaching Resources: p. 51
SAM Keyword: Survival Guide

Use with **Library Teaching Resources,** *page 50.*

Fashion Flashback
by **Richard Camden**

Genre	Pages	Lexile		Audio CD		Reading
Social Studies	16	220		10 min 23 sec		Counts!

Summary

Fashion is always changing. In the 1920s, women have fun in flapper dresses, but in the 1940s, they're serious in slacks. In the 1970s people are outrageous in platforms and bellbottoms, but prefer preppie styles in the 1980s and go grunge in the 1990s. As long as people continue to enjoy wearing clothing, styles will continue to come and go.

Phonics Focus

- *-ed* with no base change

See **Master Skills Tracker:** Teacher's Guide, page 548

Skills Tracker

Preteach Teach/Practice/Apply Review/Reinforce Assess

Smart Words

Words are defined on pp. 2–3 of the student book. Page number of first appearance is listed below.

- **decade*, p. 9**
- **fashion, p. 4**
- **popular*, p. 4**
- **practical*, p. 7**
- **trend, p. 5**

*Spanish Cognates, **page 11**

Option 1: **Decoding**

 Conference

Ask students to read the Phonics Focus words on the inside back cover of *Fashion Flashback*. If they struggle with decoding, proceed to individualized instruction.

 Individualized Instruction

For words with *-ed* with no base change: Have students use the Word Parts decoding routine on **page 18** to help students identify and use inflectional endings.

Option 2: **Vocabulary**

 Conference

Ask students to use some Smart Words listed on the inside back cover of *Fashion Flashback* in an oral sentence. Review definitions on pages 2–3 as needed. If students demonstrate proficiency, proceed to individualized instruction.

 Individualized Instruction

The idiom *show off* used in the second paragraph of page 9 means "to do something to get attention." Build understanding of idioms using the **Idioms** vocabulary routine on **page 25** with this expression as an example.

Option 3: **Fluency**

 Conference

Ask students to read page 10 of *Fashion Flashback* aloud. To work on correct phrasing, proceed to individualized instruction.

 Individualized Instruction

Use pages 10–11 of *Fashion Flashback* and the **Phrasing and Punctuation** fluency routine on **page 26** to have students practice correct phrasing.

Comprehension

Use the questions below and the Wrap-Up on **page 53** to check comprehension and promote reader response.

After Page 7: *What event makes women of the 1920s wear lighter, more fun dresses? (A big war ends in 1918, and women switch to lighter dresses so they can dance and have fun.)*

After Page 11: *What are some fashion trends in the 1970s? (long skirts, short skirts, suits with wide lapels, wide collars, high boots, platform shoes, bell-bottom jeans, skinny jeans, sparkles, bright colors, and lots of hair)*

End of Book: *What is the look of the 1990s called? (grunge)*

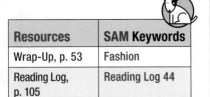

Resources	SAM Keywords
Wrap-Up, p. 53	Fashion
Reading Log, p. 105	Reading Log 44

Name _____

Fashion Flashback

Build Understanding

▶ Many styles have come and gone. Fill in the circles with some of the fashions of the past. An example is done for you.

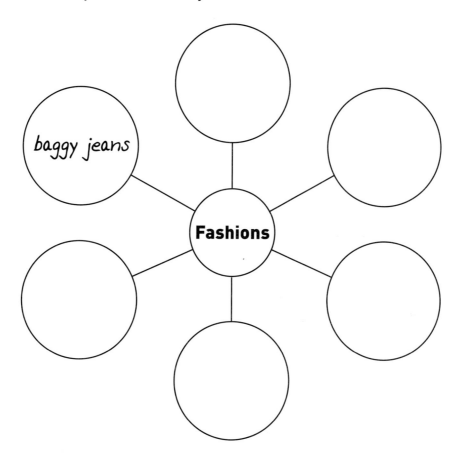

QuickWrite

▶ Which fashion from the circles above is your favorite? Describe the fashion and explain why you like it. Use details from the book to support your answer.

_____

_____

_____

Button Your Lip and Other Idioms
by **Polly Downes**

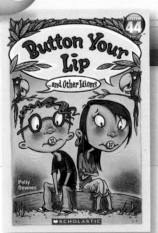

Genre	Pages	Lexile		Audio CD		Reading
Language Arts	16	210		9 min 48 sec		Counts!

Summary

Idioms are expressions that seem to mean one thing, but really mean another. This book explains what people really mean when they say, "shake a leg," "hold your horses," "put on your thinking cap," and eight other idioms.

Phonics Focus

- **Closed syllables with schwa**

See **Master Skills Tracker:** Teacher's Guide, page 548

Skills Tracker

Preteach Teach/Practice/Apply Review/Reinforce Assess

Smart Words

Words are defined on pp. 2–3 of the student book. Page number of first appearance is listed below.
- **common*, p. 4**
- **explain*, p. 4**
- **idiom, p. 4**
- **shake, p. 4**
- **tale, p. 6**

*Spanish Cognates, **page 11**

Option 1: Decoding

 Conference

Ask students to read the Phonics Focus words on the inside back cover of *Button Your Lip and Other Idioms*. If they struggle with decoding, proceed to individualized instruction.

Individualized Instruction

For words with closed syllables with schwa: Use the Syllable Strategies decoding routine on **page 16** to help students decode multisyllabic words.

Option 2: Vocabulary

 Conference

Ask students to use some Smart Words listed on the inside back cover of *Button Your Lip and Other Idioms* in an oral sentence. Review definitions on pages 2–3 as needed. If students demonstrate proficiency, proceed to individualized instruction.

Individualized Instruction

The Smart Word *explain* is the base of the words *explained, unexplained, explaining, explains, explainable, unexplainable, explanation,* and *explanatory.* Use the **Extending Meaning** vocabulary routine on **page 22** to build student familiarity with morphological word families.

Option 3: Fluency

 Conference

Ask students to read page 10 of *Button Your Lip and Other Idioms* aloud. To work on expressive reading, proceed to individualized instruction.

Individualized Instruction

Use pages 10–12 of *Button Your Lip and Other Idioms* and the **Read With Expression** fluency routine on **page 29** to have students practice expressive reading.

Comprehension

Use the questions below and the Wrap-Up on **page 55** to check comprehension and promote reader response.

After Page 6: *Where does the idiom "saved by the bell" come from?* (Hundreds of years ago, coffins had bells so that people who were buried alive could let others know.)

After Page 10: *What does the idiom "hold your horses" mean?* (Slow down and wait.)

End of Book: *Which idiom means that you've said the wrong thing at the wrong time?* (the idiom, "put your foot in your mouth")

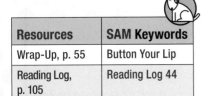

Resources	SAM Keywords
Wrap-Up, p. 55	Button Your Lip
Reading Log, p. 105	Reading Log 44

Name _____

Button Your Lip and Other Idioms

Build Understanding

▶ Match each idiom to its meaning. The first one is done for you.

1. Backseat Driver   Hurry

2. Button Your Lip   A bossy person

3. Do Not Let the Cat Out   Think about a problem
of the Bag
                                        Do not talk

4. Hit the Nail on the Head
                                        To be right

5. Hold Your Horses
                                        Slow down

6. Put on Your Thinking Cap
                                        Say the wrong thing
7. Put Your Foot in Your Mouth   at the wrong time

8. Shake a Leg   Do not tell a secret

QuickWrite

▶ Two friends are talking, and each one uses an idiom. Write what they say to
each other. Use two of the idioms above.

_____

_____

_____

African Journey

by Leslie Bakke and Susan O'Connor

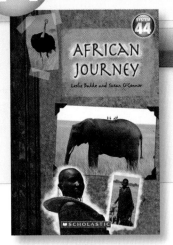

Genre	Pages	Lexile	Audio CD	Reading
Science	16	230	8 min 33 sec	Counts!

Summary

Leslie Bakke journeys to Tanzania, where she climbs Mount Kilimanjaro, the tallest mountain in Africa. She also goes on a nature safari in the Serengeti, a huge national park teeming with wildlife, and visits the Maasai, a local tribe. Her journey is recorded through a collection of vivid photos with commentary.

Phonics Focus

- **Consonant + -al, -el, or -le**

See **Master Skills Tracker:** Teacher's Guide, page 548

Skills Tracker
Preteach   Teach/Practice/Apply   Review/Reinforce   Assess

Smart Words

Words are defined on pp. 2–3 of the student book. Page number of first appearance is listed below.
- local*, p. 7
- migrate*, p. 8
- national*, p. 5
- nature*, p. 4
- travel, p. 4

*Spanish Cognates, **page 11**

Option 1: **Decoding**

Conference

Ask students to read the Phonics Focus words on the inside back cover of *African Journey*. If they struggle with decoding, proceed to individualized instruction.

Individualized Instruction

For words with consonants + -al, -el, or -le: Use the Syllable Strategies decoding routine on **page 16** to help students determine the correct vowel sounds for -al, -el, and -le.

Option 2: **Vocabulary**

Conference

Ask students to use some Smart Words listed on the inside back cover of *African Journey* in an oral sentence. Review definitions on pages 2–3 as needed. If students demonstrate proficiency, proceed to individualized instruction.

Individualized Instruction

Use the **Context Clues** vocabulary routine on **page 24** with the Smart Word *migrate* to help students use context clues to determine meaning.

Option 3: **Fluency**

Conference

Ask students to read page 8 of *African Journey* aloud. To work on correct phrasing, proceed to individualized instruction.

Individualized Instruction

Use pages 8–11 of *African Journey* and the **Phrasing and Punctuation** fluency routine on **page 26** to have students practice correct phrasing.

Comprehension

Use the questions below and the Wrap-Up on **page 57** to check comprehension and promote reader response.

After Page 7: *How long does it take Leslie to climb Mount Kilimanjaro?* (one week)

After Page 10: *The zebras look like they're hugging, but they are not. What are they doing?* (They are resting and helping each other by looking out for lions.)

End of Book: *What is the name of the tribe that Leslie visits and what do they raise?* (The tribe is called the Maasai. They raise cattle.)

Resources	SAM Keywords
Wrap-Up, p. 57	African Journey
Reading Log, p. 105	Reading Log 44

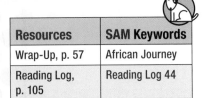

Name _____

African Journey

▶ Build Understanding

Details are bits of information. Write two details about each topic from the book. The first one is done for you.

Topic	Details
Mount Kilimanjaro (Pages 6–7)	• Mount Kilimanjaro is the tallest mountain in Africa. • There is a glacier at the top of the mountain.
Going on Safari (Pages 8–9)	
Animal Buddies (Pages 10–11)	
On the Hunt (Pages 12–13)	
Visiting the Maasai (Pages 14–15)	

QuickWrite

▶ If you could travel anywhere in the world, where would you go? What would you want to see there? Use at least one detail to support your answer.

_____

_____

_____

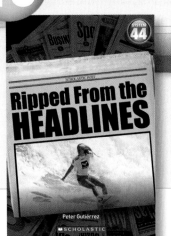

BOOK 15 Conference Guide

Ripped From the Headlines
by Peter Gutiérrez

Genre	Pages	Lexile		Audio CD		Reading
Social Studies	16	210		10 min 28 sec		Counts!

Summary

Wild stories make the headlines. Bethany makes the news after a shark bites off her arm. Felix catches a baby thrown out the window of a burning building. A hiker named Aron cuts off his own arm to save his life. These stories and others are featured in this book about brave heroes and amazing circumstances.

Phonics Focus

- Long *a* with final *e*
- Long *i* with final *e*

See **Master Skills Tracker:** Teacher's Guide, page 548

Skills Tracker

Preteach Teach/Practice/Apply Review/Reinforce Assess

Smart Words

Words are defined on pp. 2–3 of the student book. Page number of first appearance is listed below.

- amaze, p. 4
- believe, p. 4
- brave, p. 4
- danger, p. 5
- rescue*, p. 6

*Spanish Cognates, **page 11**

Option 1: **Decoding**

 Conference

Ask students to read the Phonics Focus words on the inside back cover of *Ripped From the Headlines*. If they struggle with decoding, proceed to individualized instruction.

Individualized Instruction

For words with long *a* and *i* with *final e*: Have students use the Word Sort decoding routine on **page 21** to sort words by long vowel sound. Point out that a final *e* can control a long vowel sound to make it long.

Option 2: **Vocabulary**

Conference

Ask students to use some Smart Words listed on the inside back cover of *Ripped From the Headlines* in an oral sentence. Review definitions on pages 2–3 as needed. If students demonstrate proficiency, proceed to individualized instruction.

Individualized Instruction

The Smart Word *brave* can mean "not afraid" or "to do something unpleasant and difficult," as in "He braved the storm." Use the **Multiple-Meaning Words** vocabulary routine on **page 23** with *brave* as an example to help students use context to determine the correct meaning.

Option 3: **Fluency**

 Conference

Ask students to read page 12 of *Ripped From the Headlines* aloud. To work on pacing, proceed to individualized instruction.

 Individualized Instruction

Use pages 12–13 of *Ripped From the Headlines* and the **Use Natural, Consistent Pace** fluency routine on **page 27** to have students practice reading at a natural pace.

Comprehension

Use the questions below and the Wrap-Up on **page 59** to check comprehension and promote reader response.

After Page 7: *What happens to Muhammet? (He survives after being trapped for five days under the rubble of a building.)*

After Page 9: *What happens to Palmira and who saves her? (A strange man grabs her while her gym class is outside in a park. Her friends attack the man and save her.)*

End of Book: *How does Aron's brave act save his life? (Cutting off his own arm allows him to get out from under the rock and find help.)*

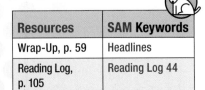

Resources	SAM Keywords
Wrap-Up, p. 59	Headlines
Reading Log, p. 105	Reading Log 44

Name _____

Ripped From the Headlines

Build Understanding

▶ Summarize each story below in your own words. One has been done for you as an example.

"Shark Attack!" *(Page 5)*

Bethany is surfing when a shark bites off her arm. A friend helps save Bethany's life. Today, Bethany is still surfing.

"Stranger Danger!" *(Pages 8–9)*

_____

_____

"Falling Baby!" *(Pages 12–13)*

_____

_____

"Trapped!" *(Pages 14-15)*

_____

_____

QuickWrite

▶ If you were Bethany or Aron, would you want to go surfing or hiking again after what happened to you? Why or why not? Explain your answer.

_____

_____

_____

BOOK 16 — Conference Guide

The Princess Brat
by **Jennifer Johnson**

Genre	Pages	Lexile	Audio CD	Reading
Fiction	16	220	8 min 35 sec	Counts!

Summary

Princess is a famous, rich brat who stars in a reality show on a ranch. For the show, she has to do chores like feeding pigs, cutting grass, and fixing lunch. She fails miserably at every job and finally quits. Back at home, she loves watching herself on TV, and her fans love to see how bratty she is.

Phonics Focus

- Soft *c* and *g*
- Suffix *-ment*

See **Master Skills Tracker:** Teacher's Guide, page 548

Skills Tracker

Preteach Teach/Practice/Apply Review/Reinforce Assess

Smart Words

Words are defined on pp. 2–3 of the student book. Page number of first appearance is listed below.

- agreement, p. 6
- famous*, p. 5
- raise, p. 4
- reality*, p. 6
- stomp, p. 8

*Spanish Cognates, **page 11**

Option 1: Decoding

Conference

Ask students to read the Phonics Focus words on the inside back cover of *The Princess Brat*. If they struggle with decoding, proceed to individualized instruction.

Individualized Instruction

For words with soft *c* and *g*: Have students use the Word Sort decoding routine on **page 21** to sort words with soft *c* and *g* spellings.

For words with suffix *-ment*: Use the Word Parts decoding routine on **page 18** to help students identify and use suffixes.

Option 2: Vocabulary

Conference

Ask students to use some Smart Words listed on the inside back cover of *The Princess Brat* in an oral sentence. Review definitions on pages 2–3 as needed. If students demonstrate proficiency, proceed to individualized instruction.

Individualized Instruction

Agree is the base of the Smart Word *agreement* and the words *agreeable*, *agreeing*, *agreements*, *disagree*, *disagreement*, and others. Use the **Extending Meaning** vocabulary routine on **page 22** to build student familiarity with morphological word families.

Option 3: Fluency

Conference

Ask students to read page 13 of *The Princess Brat* aloud. To work on natural, expressive reading proceed to individualized instruction.

Individualized Instruction

Use pages 13–14 of *The Princess Brat* and the **Read With Expression** fluency routine on **page 29** to have students practice expressive reading.

Comprehension

Use the questions below and the Wrap-Up on **page 61** to check comprehension and promote reader response.

After Page 5: *Why is Princess famous? (Nobody knows.)*

After Page 12: *Why doesn't Princess cut the grass? (It's a nice day, and she wants to relax. She feels she is working too hard.)*

End of Book: *Why do the TV fans love Princess? (They love her because she is so bratty.)*

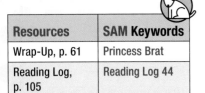

Resources	SAM Keywords
Wrap-Up, p. 61	Princess Brat
Reading Log, p. 105	Reading Log 44

Name _____

The Princess Brat

Build Understanding

▶ Fill in the circles with words that describe Princess. An example is done for you.

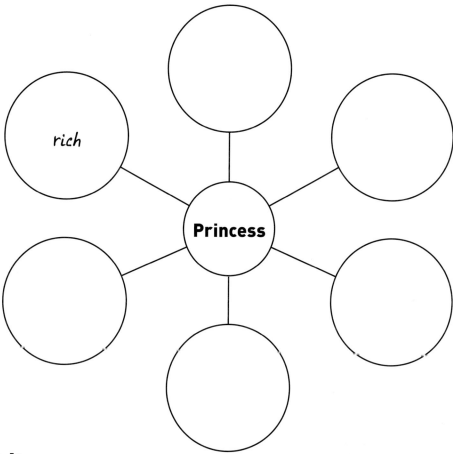

QuickWrite

▶ Would you want to be friends with Princess? Tell why or why not. Use at least one word from the circles above to support your answer.

_____

_____

_____

BOOK 17 Conference Guide

Cool Jobs in Basketball
by **Peter Gutiérrez**

Genre	Pages	Lexile	Audio CD	Reading
Jobs	16	300	9 min 51 sec	Counts!

Summary

Jobs in professional basketball aren't only for athletes. Yvonne Nelson is an intern who plans events for basketball teams. Tony Mejia is a reporter who writes about basketball. Keith Jones helps injured athletes and makes important team decisions. These individuals have found ways to use their skills and be part of basketball.

Phonics Focus

- **Words with VC*e***
- **Prefixes *non-* and *un-***

See **Master Skills Tracker:** Teacher's Guide, page 548

Skills Tracker

Preteach Teach/Practice/Apply Review/Reinforce Assess

Smart Words

Words are defined on pp. 4–5 of the student book. Page number of first appearance is listed below.
- **athlete*, p. 6**
- **business, p. 6**
- **experience*, p. 7**
- **hire, p. 6**
- **intern*, p. 8**
- **rely, p. 9**

*Spanish Cognates, **page 12**

Option 1: **Decoding**

 Conference

Ask students to read the Phonics Focus words on the inside back cover of *Cool Jobs in Basketball*. If they struggle with decoding, proceed to individualized instruction.

 Individualized Instruction

For words with VC*e*: Have students use the Word Sort decoding routine on **page 21** to sort by long *i*, *o*, and *u* sounds.

For words with prefixes *non-* and *un-*: Use the Word Parts decoding routine on **page 18** to help students identify and use prefixes.

Option 2: **Vocabulary**

 Conference

Ask students to use some Smart Words from the book in an oral sentence. Review definitions on pages 4–5 as needed. If students demonstrate proficiency, proceed to individualized instruction.

 Individualized Instruction

The Smart Word *rely* has many possible synonyms and antonyms. Use the **Extending Meaning** vocabulary routine on **page 22** to extend meaning.

Option 3: **Fluency**

 Conference

Ask students to read page 8 of *Cool Jobs in Basketball* aloud. To work on correct phrasing, proceed to individualized instruction.

 Individualized Instruction

Use pages 8–9 of *Cool Jobs in Basketball* and the **Phrasing and Punctuation** fluency routine on **page 26** to have students practice correct phrasing.

Comprehension

Use the questions below and the Wrap-Up on **page 63** to check comprehension and promote reader response.

After Chapter 1: *Why isn't professional basketball only for athletes?* (There are jobs in professional basketball for people with all kinds of experience.)

After Chapter 3: *What jobs do Yvonne and Tony have?* (Yvonne is an intern who promotes the teams and plans events. Tony writes about basketball for a Web site.)

End of Book: *How does Keith help the players he works with?* (Keith helps injured athletes by teaching them exercises to make them better.)

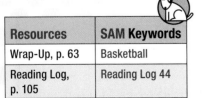

Resources	SAM Keywords
Wrap-Up, p. 63	Basketball
Reading Log, p. 105	Reading Log 44

Name _____

Cool Jobs in Basketball

Build Understanding

▶ How might Yvonne, Tony, and Keith describe their jobs? In the speech bubbles below, write what they might say. The first one is done for you.

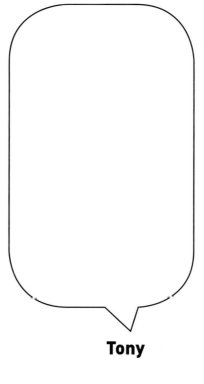

I'm an intern. I make sure the athletes look good for ads. I also plan events. I love all the friends I've made.

Yvonne

Tony

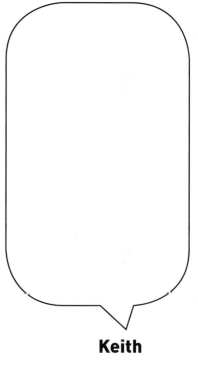

Keith

QuickWrite

▶ Which job do you think you would like most? Why? Support your answer with information from the book.

_____

_____

_____

When Lisa Met Billy
by Jorge Ramaldo

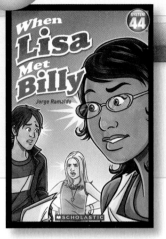

Genre	Pages	Lexile		Audio CD		Reading
Graphic Novel	16	220		9 min 22 sec		Counts!

Summary

Lisa gets the female lead in the school play. Billy, a boy Lisa likes, gets the male lead. Unfortunately, Lisa has to drop out of the play to help out at her parents' store, and Angie is given Lisa's role. Billy visits Lisa at work, and the two rehearse. When Angie gets sick, Lisa steps in to save the play and her romance with Billy.

Phonics Focus

- *–ing* with base change
- Review *–ing* with no base change

See **Master Skills Tracker:** Teacher's Guide, page 548

Skills Tracker

Preteach Teach/Practice/Apply Review/Reinforce Assess

Smart Words

Words are defined on pp. 2–3 of the student book. Page number of first appearance is listed below.

- director*, p. 5
- nervous*, p. 5
- quit, p. 9
- realize, p. 9
- rehearse, p. 5
- role*, p. 4

*Spanish Cognates, **page 12**

Option 1: Decoding

Conference

Ask students to read the Phonics Focus words on the inside back cover of *When Lisa Met Billy*. If they struggle with decoding, proceed to individualized instruction.

Individualized Instruction

For words with *–ing* with and without base change: Use the Word Parts decoding routine on **page 18** to help students identify and use inflectional endings.

Option 2: Vocabulary

Conference

Ask students to use some Smart Words listed on the inside back cover of *When Lisa Met Billy* in an oral sentence. Review definitions on pages 2–3 as needed. If students demonstrate proficiency, proceed to individualized instruction.

Individualized Instruction

The Smart Word *quit* has many possible synonyms and antonyms. Use the **Extending Meaning** vocabulary routine on **page 22** to extend meaning.

Option 3: Fluency

Conference

Ask students to read page 6 of *When Lisa Met Billy* aloud. To work on expressive reading, proceed to individualized instruction.

Individualized Instruction

Use pages 6–9 of *When Lisa Met Billy* and the **Read With Expression** fluency routine on **page 29** to have students practice expressive reading.

Comprehension

Use the questions below and the Wrap-Up on **page 65** to check comprehension and promote reader response.

After page 7: *What role does Lisa get in the play?* (She gets the part of Rosita, the lead role.)

After page 10: *What two things is Lisa upset about?* (She is upset because she can't be in the play. She's also upset because she won't get to spend time with Billy.)

End of Book: *Why does Lisa get another chance to be in the play?* (Angie gets sick and Lisa knows Rosita's lines because she has been practicing with Billy.)

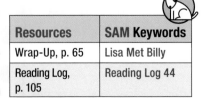

Resources	SAM Keywords
Wrap-Up, p. 65	Lisa Met Billy
Reading Log, p. 105	Reading Log 44

Name _____

When Lisa Met Billy

Build Understanding

▶ Fill in the solution to each problem below. Use details from the book.
One has been done for you.

Problem	Solution
1. Lisa gets a part in the play, but her parents tell her they need her help in the store.	*Lisa quits the play.*
2. Lisa has to work, but she wants to find a way to see Billy.	
3. Angie gets sick. She can't be in the play.	

QuickWrite

▶ Why does Billy want to rehearse with Lisa when she's not even in the play?
Tell what you think. Support your answer with details from the story.

_____

_____

_____

Crash!
by **Steph Smith**

Genre	Pages	Lexile	Audio CD	Reading Counts!
Science	16	320	10 min 12 sec	

Summary

Scientists are keeping track of asteroids, especially one named Apophis. Experts tracking Apophis know that in the future it will fly by Earth. If Apophis crashes into Earth, it will create tremendous damage. Scientists have some ideas about how to knock an asteroid off its path. They just hope it won't get too close!

Phonics Focus

- *-ed* with no base change
- *-ed* with base change
- *y* as a vowel

See **Master Skills Tracker:** Teacher's Guide, page 548

Skills Tracker

Preteach | Teach/Practice/Apply | Review/Reinforce | Assess

Smart Words

Words are defined on pp. 4–5 of the student book. Page number of first appearance is listed below.

- expert*, p. 7
- follow, p. 7
- gravity*, p. 12
- orbit*, p. 10
- telescope*, p. 10

*Spanish Cognates, **page 12**

Option 1: Decoding

Conference

Ask students to read the Phonics Focus words on the inside back cover of *Crash!* If they struggle with decoding, proceed to individualized instruction.

Individualized Instruction

For words with *-ed* with and without base change: Use the Word Parts decoding routine on **page 18** to help students identify and use inflectional endings.

For words with *y* as a vowel: Have students use the Word Sort decoding routine on **page 21** to sort words by long *e*, long *i*, and short *i* sounds.

Option 2: Vocabulary

Conference

Ask students to use some Smart Words from the book in an oral sentence. Review definitions on pages 4–5 as needed. If students demonstrate proficiency, proceed to individualized instruction.

Individualized Instruction

The Smart Word *follow* can mean "to watch or keep track of something as it moves" or "to chase or pursue." Use the **Multiple-Meaning Words** vocabulary routine on **page 23** with *follow* as an example to help students determine the correct meaning.

Option 3: Fluency

Conference

Ask students to read page 10 of *Crash!* aloud. To work on expressive reading, proceed to individualized instruction.

Individualized Instruction

Use pages 10–11 of *Crash!* and the **Read With Expression** fluency routine on **page 29** to have students practice expressive reading.

Comprehension

Use the questions below and the Wrap-Up on **page 67** to check comprehension and promote reader response.

After Chapter 1: *What is an asteroid? (It is a big rock that flies around in space.)*

After Chapter 2: *What ideas do experts have about how to stop an asteroid from hitting Earth? (The asteroid can be pushed away by a spaceship that crashes into it. Or, it can be pulled away using the force of gravity from a big ship.)*

End of Book: *When Apophis flies by Earth again in 2029, where will be the best place to see it? (The best place to see it will be in Europe.)*

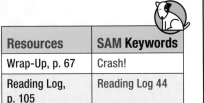

Resources	SAM Keywords
Wrap-Up, p. 67	Crash!
Reading Log, p. 105	Reading Log 44

Name _____

Crash!

Build Understanding

▶ Identify the most important ideas in each chapter. Then, summarize the chapter in your own words. One has been done for you as an example.

Chapter 1: "Look! An Asteroid!"

_____

_____

_____

Chapter 2: "On the Right Track"

An asteroid named Apophis could hit Earth. Scientists are studying

it and tracking it. Experts have ideas about how to throw an asteroid

off track to prevent it from slamming into Earth.

Chapter 3: "Out of This World"

_____

_____

_____

QuickWrite

▶ Should people be worried about Apophis hitting Earth? Tell why or why not. Use details from the book.

_____

_____

_____

Resource Links
Library Teaching Resources: p. 67
SAM Keyword: Crash!

Use with **Library Teaching Resources,** *page 66.*

System 44 Library **67**

Back From the Grave!

Based on a Story by Guy de Maupassant

Adapted by **Michael Leviton**

| Genre
Classic Retelling | Pages
16 | Lexile
240 | Audio CD
9 min 45 sec | Reading
Counts! |

Summary

After Juliet dies, her father is awakened by the doorbell and finds her at the door. A grave robber had cut off her fingers to steal her rings and woken her from her death-like sleep. Their servant, the robber, drops dead at the sight of Juliet. Juliet is grateful to him, for otherwise she would still be in the coffin.

Phonics Focus

- Suffixes *-y* and *-ly*
- Change *y* to *i*

See **Master Skills Tracker:** Teacher's Guide, page 548

Skills Tracker

Preteach | Teach/Practice/Apply | Review/Reinforce | Assess

Smart Words

Words are defined on pp. 4–5 of the student book. Page number of first appearance is listed below.

- **bury, p. 9**
- **coffin, p. 10**
- **dream, p. 11**
- **examine*, p. 8**
- **remove, p. 9**
- **worry, p. 8**

*Spanish Cognates, **page 12**

Option 1: Decoding

 Conference

Ask students to read the Phonics Focus words on the inside back cover of *Back From the Grave!* If they struggle with decoding, proceed to individualized instruction.

 Individualized Instruction

For words with suffixes -y and -ly, and words in which y changes to i: Use the Word Parts decoding routine on **page 18** to help students identify and use suffixes and inflectional endings.

Option 2: Vocabulary

 Conference

Ask students to use some Smart Words from the book in an oral sentence. Review definitions on pages 4–5 as needed. If students demonstrate proficiency, proceed to individualized instruction.

 Individualized Instruction

The Smart Word *remove* has many possible synonyms and antonyms. Use the **Extending Meaning** vocabulary routine on **page 22** to extend meaning.

Option 3: Fluency

 Conference

Ask students to read page 14 of *Back From the Grave!* aloud. To work on expressive reading, proceed to individualized instruction.

 Individualized Instruction

Use pages 14–15 of *Back From the Grave!* and the **Read With Expression** fluency routine on **page 29** to have students practice expressive reading.

Comprehension

Use the questions below and the Wrap-Up on **page 69** to check comprehension and promote reader response.

After Chapter 1: *What gift does Juliet receive from her father?* (She receives four rings with red stones.)

After Chapter 3: *What happens the night after Juliet is buried?* (Juliet's father has a dream in which Juliet is crying that she isn't dead. Then the doorbell rings, and standing at the door is a bloody girl who claims to be Juliet.)

End of Book: *Why is Juliet grateful to Prosper?* (She says that if he hadn't robbed her, she'd still be buried alive.)

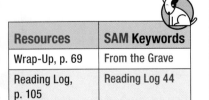

Resources	SAM Keywords
Wrap-Up, p. 69	From the Grave
Reading Log, p. 105	Reading Log 44

Name _____

Back From the Grave!

Build Understanding

▶ Answer the questions below using details from the story. The first one is done for you.

Chapter 1: "Juliet's Death"
What does Juliet die from?

She dies from a weak heart.

Chapter 2: "Sad Good-Byes"
What does Juliet's best friend say about Juliet?

Chapter 3: "The Visitor"
What does Juliet's father see when he opens the door in the middle of the night?

Chapter 4: "Dead or Alive?"
What does Prosper do to Juliet?

QuickWrite

▶ Prosper does a shocking thing. But something good comes out of it. Write at least two sentences to explain how this happens.

_____

_____

_____

BOOK 21 Conference Guide

El Tiburón
by Patrick Daley

Genre	Pages	Lexile	Audio CD	Reading
Social Studies	16	340	9 min 57 sec	Counts!

Summary

Sergio is paralyzed after a terrible car accident. At first he is depressed, but he finds purpose for his life by training to be a long-distance swimmer. With determination and support from his brother Marcos, he swims the Strait of Gibraltar and becomes famous.

Phonics Focus

- Silent letters *wr-* and *-mb*
- *ph*
- Digraph *wh-*
- Review endings *-ed, -ing*

See **Master Skills Tracker:**
Teacher's Guide, page 548

Skills Tracker

Preteach Teach/Practice/Apply Review/Reinforce Assess

Smart Words

Words are defined on pp. 4–5 of the student book. Page number of first appearance is listed below.

- accident*, p. 6
- attempt, p. 9
- complete*, p. 12
- hope, p. 8
- purpose*, p. 9
- support, p. 9

*Spanish Cognates, **page 12**

Option 1: **Decoding**

 Conference

Ask students to read the Phonics Focus words on the inside back cover of *El Tiburón*. If they struggle with decoding, proceed to individualized instruction.

Individualized Instruction

For words with digraph *wh-*: Use the Blends and Digraphs decoding routine on **page 17** to help students build accuracy.

For words with *-ed* and *-ing*: Use the Word Parts decoding routine on **page 18** to help students identify and use inflectional endings.

Option 2: **Vocabulary**

 Conference

Ask students to use some Smart Words from the book in an oral sentence. Review definitions on pages 4–5 as needed. If students demonstrate proficiency, proceed to individualized instruction.

 Individualized Instruction

The Smart Word *support* is the base of the words *supporters*, *supportive*, and *supporting*. Use the Extending Meaning vocabulary routine on **page 22** to build student familiarity with morphological word families.

Option 3: **Fluency**

 Conference

Ask students to read page 8 of *El Tiburón* aloud. To practice correct phrasing, proceed to individualized instruction.

 Individualized Instruction

Use pages 8–9 of *El Tiburón* and the **Phrasing and Punctuation** fluency routine on **page 26** to have students practice correct phrasing.

Comprehension

Use the questions below and the Wrap-Up on **page 71** to check comprehension and promote reader response.

After Chapter 1: *What happens to Sergio? (He becomes paralyzed in a car accident and can't walk.)*

After Chapter 2: *What makes Sergio happy again? (He becomes a long-distance swimmer and feels he has a purpose again.)*

End of Book: *Why does Sergio become famous? (He is the first disabled person to swim the Strait of Gibraltar.)*

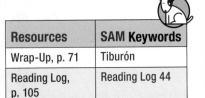

Resources	SAM Keywords
Wrap-Up, p. 71	Tiburón
Reading Log, p. 105	Reading Log 44

Name _____

El Tiburón

Build Understanding

▶ Events from the story are listed in the box. Write each event in the order it occurs in the story. The first one is done for you.

Events
Sergio hires a swimming coach.
Sergio swims for 24 hours in Marcos's honor.
Sergio breaks his spine.
Sergio swims the Strait of Gibraltar.
Sergio dreams that the ocean speaks to him.

First
Sergio breaks his spine.

⬇

Second

⬇

Next

⬇

Then

⬇

Last

QuickWrite

▶ Do you think Sergio is a hero? Why or why not? Write a sentence that explains your opinion. Use details from the book to support your answer.

_____

_____

_____

Resource Links
Library Teaching Resources: p. 71
SAM Keyword: Tiburón

Use with **Library Teaching Resources,** *page 70.*

Medical Miracle

by **Allison Langley**

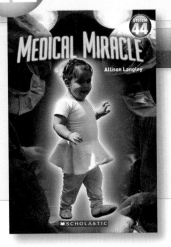

Genre	Pages	Lexile	Audio CD	Reading Counts!
Science	16	340	9 min 32 sec	✓

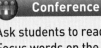

Summary

Milagros is born with mermaid syndrome, a condition in which the legs are fused together like a mermaid's tail. Her parents appeal for help, and Dr. Luis Rubio agrees to perform the difficult surgery for free. People across Peru watch the surgery live on TV. Milagros still needs other surgeries, but today she is able to walk.

Phonics Focus

- **Open syllables**
- **Unstressed open syllables**

See **Master Skills Tracker:** Teacher's Guide, page 548

Skills Tracker

Preteach Teach/Practice/Apply Review/Reinforce Assess

Smart Words

Words are defined on pp. 4–5 of the student book. Page number of first appearance is listed below.

- artery*, p. 9
- fused*, p. 6
- prepare*, p. 10
- stretch, p. 10
- surgery*, p. 9
- syndrome*, p. 7

*Spanish Cognates, **page 12**

Option 1: **Decoding**

 Conference

Ask students to read the Phonics Focus words on the inside back cover of *Medical Miracle*. If they struggle with decoding, proceed to individualized instruction.

Individualized Instruction

For words with open syllables and unstressed open syllables: Use the Syllable Strategies routine on **page 16** to help students determine the correct vowel sounds in unstressed open syllables.

Option 2: **Vocabulary**

Conference

Ask students to use some Smart Words listed on the inside back cover of *Medical Miracle* in an oral sentence. Review definitions on pages 4–5 as needed. If students demonstrate proficiency, proceed to individualized instruction.

Individualized Instruction

Use the **Context Clues** vocabulary routine on **page 24** with the Smart Word *artery* to help students use context clues to determine meaning.

Option 3: **Fluency**

 Conference

Ask students to read page 6 of *Medical Miracle* aloud. To work on pacing, proceed to individualized instruction.

Individualized Instruction

Use pages 6–8 of *Medical Miracle* and the **Use Natural, Consistent Pace** fluency routine on **page 27** to have students practice reading at a natural pace.

Comprehension

Use the questions below and the Wrap-Up on **page 73** to check comprehension and promote reader response.

After Chapter 1: *What makes Milagros different from other babies?* (She is born with her legs fused together.)

After Chapter 2: *Why does Dr. Rubio put balloons under Milagros's skin?* (He does this to stretch her skin so that there will be enough skin to cover both legs after they are separated.)

End of Book: *Why is Milagros a medical miracle?* (She makes it through the surgery and has another successful operation a year later. Most children born like her die after birth.)

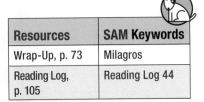

Resources	SAM Keywords
Wrap-Up, p. 73	Milagros
Reading Log, p. 105	Reading Log 44

Name _____

Medical Miracle

Build Understanding

▶ Milagros's parents and doctor face many problems in trying to help her. Fill in the solution to each problem listed below. The first one is done for you.

Problem	Solution
1. Milagros is born with her two legs fused together. [Chapter 1]	*Milagros needs an operation to separate her legs.*
2. Sara and Ricardo have no money to help their baby. [Chapter 1]	
3. Milagros doesn't have enough skin to cover both legs. [Chapter 2]	
4. Milagros has weak kidneys and feet that are not straight. [Chapter 3]	

QuickWrite

▶ Why do you think the people of Peru want to know about Milagros and her surgery? Explain your answer with details from the book.

_____

_____

_____

Disaster!
by **Sean Price**

Genre	Pages	Lexile	Audio CD	Reading
Science	**24**	**330**	**13 min 35 sec**	**Counts!**

Summary

When tornadoes, tsunamis, and hurricanes strike, the result is often disaster. In 1999, tornadoes roar through Oklahoma and other states. In 2004, a tsunami in the Indian Ocean kills over 280,000 people. In 2005, Hurricane Katrina causes the New Orleans levees to break, flooding the city. Read how survivors of these disasters rebuild their homes and their lives.

Phonics Focus

- *com-* and *con-*

See **Master Skills Tracker:** Teacher's Guide, page 548

Skills Tracker

Preteach   Teach/Practice/Apply   Review/Reinforce   Assess

Smart Words

Words are defined on pp. 4–5 of the student book. Page number of first appearance is listed below.

- aid, p. 16
- damage, p. 6
- escape*, p. 14
- massive*, p. 12
- survivor, p. 16
- warning, p. 10

*Spanish Cognates, **page 13**

Option 1: **Decoding**

 Conference

Ask students to read the Phonics Focus words on the inside back cover of *Disaster!* If they struggle with decoding, proceed to individualized instruction.

Individualized Instruction

For words with *com-* and *con-*: Use the Word Parts decoding routine on **page 18** to help students identify and use prefixes.

Option 2: **Vocabulary**

 Conference

Ask students to use some Smart Words listed on the inside back cover of *Disaster!* in an oral sentence. Review definitions on pages 4–5 as needed. If students demonstrate proficiency, proceed to individualized instruction.

Individualized Instruction

The Smart Word *aid* has many possible synonyms and antonyms. Use the **Extending Meaning** vocabulary routine on **page 22** to extend meaning.

Option 3: **Fluency**

 Conference

Ask students to read page 6 of *Disaster!* aloud. To work on pacing, proceed to individualized instruction.

Individualized Instruction

Use pages 6–8 of *Disaster!* and the **Use Natural, Consistent Pace** fluency routine on **page 27** to have students practice correct pacing.

Comprehension

Use the questions below and the Wrap-Up on **page 75** to check comprehension and promote reader response.

After Chapter 1: *What happens to Kaci's home during the tornado?* (The power goes out, the outer walls shake apart, and then the roof flies off.)

After Chapter 2: *What kind of damage does the 2004 tsunami cause?* (It kills at least 280,000 people and leaves survivors homeless.)

End of Book: *What happens to the levees in New Orleans?* (They break and water pours in, flooding most of New Orleans.)

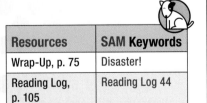

Resources	SAM Keywords
Wrap-Up, p. 75	Disaster!
Reading Log, p. 105	Reading Log 44

Name _____

Disaster!

Build Understanding

▶ Kaci, Fitri, and Troy all survive disasters. Imagine that they can all speak to each other. What would they tell each other about their experiences? Write what they would say.

1. Kaci *(Chapter 1)*   **2. Fitri** *(Chapter 2)*   **3. Troy** *(Chapter 3)*

QuickWrite

▶ After the tsunami hits, many people help Fitri and other victims. What do you think you could do to help a victim of a natural disaster? Write some ideas below.

_____

_____

_____

The Sweater Thief
by **Ayana Carter**

Genre	Pages	Lexile	Audio CD	Reading
Fiction	**24**	**250**	**12 min 36 sec**	**Counts!**

Summary

Tracey's job at an expensive clothing store goes well until Kayla, a popular girl from school, pressures Tracey into letting her steal a sweater. Kayla invites Tracey to a party. Tracey goes, but is plagued by guilt. When Kayla returns to the store and steals again, Tracey tells her boss and learns a lesson about who her real friends are.

Phonics Focus

- **Long *a* vowel teams**

See **Master Skills Tracker:**
Teacher's Guide, page 548

Skills Tracker

Preteach Teach/Practice/Apply Review/Reinforce Assess

Smart Words

Words are defined on pp. 4–5 of the student book. Page number of first appearance is listed below.

- confused*, p. 12
- employee*, p. 8
- expensive, p. 6
- ignore*, p. 13
- include*, p. 13
- praise, p. 8

*Spanish Cognates, **page 13**

Option 1: **Decoding**

 Conference

Ask students to read the Phonics Focus words on the inside back cover of *The Sweater Thief*. If they struggle with decoding, proceed to individualized instruction.

 Individualized Instruction

For words with long *a* vowel teams: Have students use the Word Sort decoding routine on **page 21** to sort words by *ai* and *ay* spellings. Review that both spellings stand for the long *a* sound.

Option 2: **Vocabulary**

 Conference

Ask students to use some Smart Words listed on the inside back cover of *The Sweater Thief* in an oral sentence. Review definitions on pages 4–5 as needed. If students demonstrate proficiency, proceed to individualized instruction.

 Individualized Instruction

Employ is the base of the Smart Word *employee* and the words *employed*, *employees*, *employer*, *employers*, *employing*, *employment*, and *employs*. Use the **Extending Meaning** vocabulary routine on **page 22** to build student familiarity with morphological word families.

Option 3: **Fluency**

 Conference

Ask students to read page 9 of *The Sweater Thief* aloud. To work on pacing, proceed to individualized instruction.

 Individualized Instruction

Use pages 9–12 of *The Sweater Thief* and the **Use Natural, Consistent Pace** fluency routine on **page 27** to have students practice reading at a natural pace.

Comprehension

Use the questions below and the Wrap-Up on **page 77** to check comprehension and promote reader response.

After Chapter 1: *What does Tracey like about her job? (She likes her boss, and she likes being praised.)*

After Chapter 3: *What happens the second time that Kayla comes into the store? (The alarm goes off. Inez asks Tracey to check out the situation. Tracey sees that Kayla is trying to steal a sweater and lets Kayla steal it.)*

End of Book: *What does Tracey realize about Kayla? (She realizes that Kayla is using her and isn't a person worth being friends with.)*

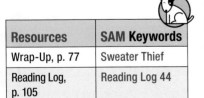

Resources	SAM Keywords
Wrap-Up, p. 77	Sweater Thief
Reading Log, p. 105	Reading Log 44

Name _____

The Sweater Thief

Build Understanding

▶ Imagine that Tracey and Kayla have a chance to speak to each other now. What would they say? Fill in the speech bubbles. Use what you know about both girls to predict what they might say to each other.

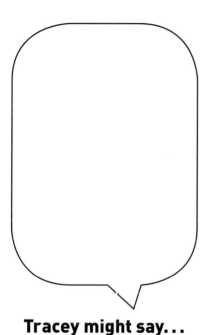

Tracey might say...

Kayla might say...

QuickWrite

▶ Do you think Tracey is an honest person? Why or why not? Use what you've written in the speech bubbles above and details from the story to support your opinion.

_____

_____

_____

BOOK 25 · Conference Guide

Left to Die
by **Nancy Honovich**

Genre	Pages	Lexile	Audio CD	Reading
Science	24	350	15 min 31 sec	Counts!

Summary

Joe and Simon challenge themselves to a dangerous mountain climb up the Siula Grande in Peru. They reach the top successfully, but Joe breaks his leg on the climb down. Simon lowers Joe down the mountain with a rope, but then Joe falls into a crevasse. Sure that Joe is dead, Simon leaves him behind to save himself. Joe crawls out of the crevasse back to camp. He shocks Simon, who can't believe Joe is still alive.

Phonics Focus

- **Long *o* vowel teams *oa* and *ow***

See **Master Skills Tracker:** Teacher's Guide, page 548

Skills Tracker

Preteach | Teach/Practice/Apply | Review/Reinforce | Assess

Smart Words

Words are defined on pp. 4–5 of the student book. Page number of first appearance is listed below.

- approach, p. 8
- gear, p. 8
- glacier*, p. 7
- struggle, p. 15
- summit, p. 8
- vertical*, p. 6

*Spanish Cognates, **page 13**

Option 1: **Decoding**

Conference

Ask students to read the Phonics Focus words on the inside back cover of *Left to Die*. If they struggle with decoding, proceed to individualized instruction.

Individualized Instruction

For words with long *o* vowel teams *oa* and *ow*: Have students use the Word Sort decoding routine on **page 21** to sort words by *oa* and *ow* spellings. Review that both spellings can stand for the long *o* sound.

Option 2: **Vocabulary**

Conference

Ask students to use some Smart Words from the book in an oral sentence. Review definitions on pages 4–5 as needed. If students demonstrate proficiency, proceed to individualized instruction.

Individualized Instruction

Use the **Context Clues** vocabulary routine on **page 24** with the Smart Word *vertical* as an example to help students use context clues to determine meaning.

Option 3: **Fluency**

Conference

Ask students to read page 14 of *Left to Die* aloud. To practice expressive reading, proceed to individualized instruction.

Individualized Instruction

Use pages 14–15 of *Left to Die* and the **Read With Expression** fluency routine on **page 29** to have students practice reading in a varied, expressive tone.

Comprehension

Use the questions below and the Wrap-Up on **page 79** to check comprehension and promote reader response.

After Chapter 1: *Why is Siula Grande such a dangerous mountain to climb?* (The mountain's West Face is almost vertical, and a glacier with crevasses covers part of the mountain.)

After Chapter 4: *Why does Simon cut the rope?* (He knows that if he doesn't cut it, he will be pulled off the mountain.)

End of Book: *How does Joe make it back to camp?* (He crawls for days.)

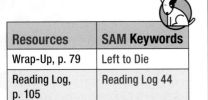

Resources	SAM Keywords
Wrap-Up, p. 79	Left to Die
Reading Log, p. 105	Reading Log 44

Name ______________________________

Left to Die

Build Understanding

▶ Joe and Simon face many problems on their climb. Fill in the chart below with the solution to each problem. An example has been done for you.

Problem	Solution
1. Joe breaks his leg. *(Page 14)*	Simon lowers Joe down by ropes.
2. The heavy rope starts to pull Simon down. *(Page 18)*	
3. Joe can't climb up the ice walls of the crevasse. *(Pages 19-20)*	
4. Joe has to get back to camp. *(Page 21)*	

QuickWrite

▶ Which problem or challenge that Joe faces would scare you the most? Why? Use details from the book to support your answer.

____

____

____

Resource Links
Library Teaching Resources: p. 79
SAM Keyword: Left to Die

Use with **Library Teaching Resources,** *page 78.*

Samurai Fighters
by **Mel Friedman**

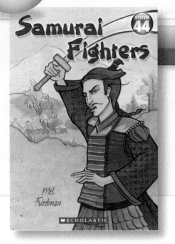

Genre	Pages	Lexile	Audio CD	Reading
Social Studies	**24**	**300**	**15 min 46 sec**	**Counts!**

Summary

The first Japanese samurai are warriors who serve and fight for the rich. Eventually, samurai gain independence. Their leader, the shogun, becomes more powerful than the emperor of Japan. Skilled samurai like the swordswoman Tomoe become legends. The shogun brings peace to Japan, but this creates less need for samurai. Unemployed samurai, called ronin, must find other work. Musashi is the last great samurai.

Phonics Focus

- **Long *e* vowel teams *ea*, *ee*, and *ie***

See **Master Skills Tracker:** Teacher's Guide, page 548

Skills Tracker

Preteach Teach/Practice/Apply Review/Reinforce Assess

Smart Words

Words are defined on pp. 4–5 of the student book. Page number of first appearance is listed below.

- clan*, p. 7
- defeat, p. 9
- emperor*, p. 8
- enemy*, p. 9
- legend*, p. 8
- samurai*, p. 7

*Spanish Cognates, **page 13**

Option 1: **Decoding**

Conference

Ask students to read the Phonics Focus words on the inside back cover of *Samurai Fighters*. If they struggle with decoding, proceed to individualized instruction.

Individualized Instruction

For words with vowel teams *ea*, *ee*, and *ie*: Have students use the Word Sort decoding routine on **page 21** to sort words by *ee*, *ea*, and *ie* spellings. Review that all three spellings can stand for the long *e* sound.

Option 2: **Vocabulary**

Conference

Ask students to use some Smart Words listed on the inside back cover of *Samurai Fighters* in an oral sentence. Review definitions on pages 4–5 as needed. If students demonstrate proficiency, proceed to individualized instruction.

Individualized Instruction

Use the **Context Clues** vocabulary routine on **page 24** with the Smart Word *legend* as an example to help students use context clues to determine meaning.

Option 3: **Fluency**

Conference

Ask students to read page 7 of *Samurai Fighters* aloud. To work on pacing, proceed to individualized instruction.

Individualized Instruction

Use pages 7–9 of *Samurai Fighters* and the **Use Natural, Consistent Pace** fluency routine on **page 27** to have students practice correct pacing.

Comprehension

Use the questions below and the Wrap-Up on **page 81** to check comprehension and promote reader response.

After Chapter 1: *Why do Yoshiie's fighters respect him more than the emperor?* (The emperor refuses to pay them, but Yoshiie rewards them.)

After Chapter 3: *Who are the ronin, and what do they do to make money?* (Ronin are former samurai who try to make money in other ways.)

End of Book: *Why does Musashi become a legend?* (He is never defeated in battle. His book about sword fighting is still read today.)

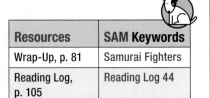

Resources	SAM Keywords
Wrap-Up, p. 81	Samurai Fighters
Reading Log, p. 105	Reading Log 44

Name _____

Samurai Fighters

Build Understanding

▶ Fill in the circles with details that tell about the samurai. You may describe their skills, behavior, clothing, and jobs. An example has been done for you.

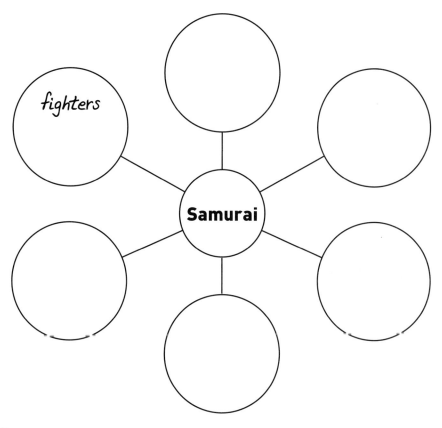

QuickWrite

▶ It's time to hire a new samurai. Write a job ad that describes the skills needed. Use at least two details from the book in your description.

_____

_____

_____

BOOK 27 Conference Guide

Ant Attack!

Based on the short story "Leiningen Versus the Ants" by Carl Stephenson

Adapted by **Michael Leviton**

Genre	Pages	Lexile		Audio CD		Reading
Classic Retelling	24	290		16 min		Counts!

Summary

Rodriguez is warned that killer ants will invade his farm. Instead of leaving, he digs two ditches. He fills one with water and the other with fire. The ants find a way to cross the water and wait out the fire, so Rodriguez decides to open a dam and flood his farm to drown the ants. Although Rodriguez stops the invasion, the ants nearly kill him.

Phonics Focus

- Prefixes *pre-* and *re-*
- Long *i igh*
- Other long *i* spellings
- Other long *o* spellings

See **Master Skills Tracker:** Teacher's Guide, page 548

Skills Tracker

Preteach Teach/Practice/Apply Review/Reinforce Assess

Smart Words

Words are defined on pp. 4–5 of the student book. Page number of first appearance is listed below.

- attack*, p. 8
- drown, p. 10
- horror*, p. 10
- invade*, p. 6
- precaution*, p. 9
- reassure, p. 9

*Spanish Cognates, **page 13**

Option 1: **Decoding**

 Conference

Ask students to read the Phonics Focus words on the inside back cover of *Ant Attack!* If they struggle with decoding, proceed to individualized instruction.

 Individualized Instruction

For words with prefixes *pre-* and *re-*: Use the Word Parts decoding routine on **page 18** to help students identify and use prefixes.

For words with long *i* and *o* spellings: Have students use the Word Sort decoding routine on **page 21** to sort words by long *i* and long *o* sounds.

Option 2: **Vocabulary**

 Conference

Ask students to use some Smart Words from the book in an oral sentence. Review definitions on pages 4–5 as needed. If students demonstrate proficiency, proceed to individualized instruction.

 Individualized Instruction

Use the **Context Clues** vocabulary routine on **page 24** with the Smart Word *precaution* as an example to help students use context clues to determine meaning.

Option 3: **Fluency**

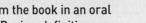

 Conference

Ask students to read page 18 of *Ant Attack!* aloud. To work on expressive reading, proceed to individualized instruction.

 Individualized Instruction

Use pages 18–19 of *Ant Attack!* and the **Read With Expression** fluency routine on **page 29** to have students practice expressive reading.

Comprehension

Use the questions below and the Wrap-Up on **page 83** to check comprehension and promote reader response.

After Chapter 1: *Why doesn't Rodriguez listen to the man who comes to warn him?* (Rodriguez thinks it's ridiculous to be afraid of ants.)

After Chapter 4: *Why don't the two ditches keep the ants away?* (The ants cross the first ditch by walking on each other. The fire in the second ditch will eventually burn out.)

End of Book: *How does Rodriguez finally stop the ant attack?* (He opens up a dam that floods the farm and kills the ants.)

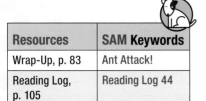

Resources	SAM Keywords
Wrap-Up, p. 83	Ant Attack!
Reading Log, p. 105	Reading Log 44

Name _____

Ant Attack!

Build Understanding

▶ Read the list of events below. Then write the events in the order in which they happen in the book. The first one is done for you.

Events
Rodriguez runs to open up the dam.
A man on a boat warns Rodriguez about the killer ants.
Workers pick the ants off Rodriguez and carry him to the barn roof.
The workers build two ditches.
Rodriguez ignites the gas to make a wall of fire.

First *A man on a boat warns Rodriguez about the killer ants.*

Second

Third

Fourth

Last

QuickWrite

▶ Imagine you are working on Rodriguez's farm during the ant attack. Do you like Rodriguez, or are you mad at him? Write your opinion and give at least one reason for it.

_____

_____

_____

Resource Links
Library Teaching Resources: p. 83
SAM Keyword: Ant Attack!

Use with **Library Teaching Resources,** *page 82.*

System 44 Library **83**

Witch Hunt
by **Carol Domblewski**

Genre	Pages	Lexile	Audio CD	Reading
Social Studies	24	300	15 min 27 sec	Counts!

Summary

In 1692 in Salem, Massachusetts, two girls claim that witches have put a spell on them. The girls accuse three women of being witches. The women are arrested. More girls accuse people of witchcraft. The fear of being accused spreads. Innocent people are arrested and hung. Finally, people speak out against the arrests and stop the madness.

Phonics Focus

- **Multiple affixes**
- **Ending -ed with base change**
- **Suffixes -ly and -y**

See **Master Skills Tracker:** Teacher's Guide, page 548

Skills Tracker			
Preteach	Teach/Practice/Apply	Review/Reinforce	Assess

Smart Words

Words are defined on pp. 4–5 of the student book. Page number of first appearance is listed below.

- **accuse*, p. 6**
- **admit*, p. 10**
- **hearing, p. 13**
- **release, p. 22**
- **rumor*, p. 9**
- **trial, p. 19**

*Spanish Cognates, **page 13**

Option 1: **Decoding**

 Conference

Ask students to read the Phonics Focus words on the inside back cover of *Witch Hunt*. If they struggle with decoding, proceed to individualized instruction.

Individualized Instruction

For words with multiple affixes, -ed with base change, and suffixes -ly and -y: Use the Word Parts decoding routine on **page 18** to help students identify and use prefixes, suffixes, and inflectional endings.

Option 2: **Vocabulary**

 Conference

Ask students to use some Smart Words from the book in an oral sentence. Review definitions on pages 4–5 as needed. If students demonstrate proficiency, proceed to individualized instruction.

 Individualized Instruction

The Smart Word *hearing* can mean "perceiving sound" or "a court trial." Use the **Multiple-Meaning Words** vocabulary routine on **page 23** with *hearing* as an example to help students use context to determine the correct meaning.

Option 3: **Fluency**

 Conference

Ask students to read page 13 of *Witch Hunt* aloud. To work on reading with correct phrasing, proceed to individualized instruction.

 Individualized Instruction

Use pages 13–15 of *Witch Hunt* and the **Phrasing and Punctuation** fluency routine on **page 26** to have students practice correct phrasing.

Comprehension

Use the questions below and the Wrap-Up on **page 85** to check comprehension and promote reader response.

After Chapter 1: *What does the doctor say is the reason the girls are having strange fits?* (He says that the girls are under a spell.)

After Chapter 3: *What happens to the people who are accused of being witches?* (They are taken before a judge who tries to get them to admit that they are witches.)

End of Book: *What do some people do to help end the Salem witch trials?* (Increase Mather says it is wrong to hang innocent people. Thomas Brattle says there is no real proof that people are witches. The governor shuts down the trials.)

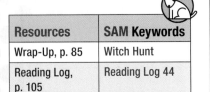

Resources	SAM Keywords
Wrap-Up, p. 85	Witch Hunt
Reading Log, p. 105	Reading Log 44

Name _____

Witch Hunt

Build Understanding

▶ Write a short summary of each chapter of the book. One has been done for you.

Chapter 1: "Scary Rumors"

_____

_____

Chapter 2: "Arrested!"

_____

_____

Chapter 3: "Fear Takes Over"

Three accused women are brought before a judge. Two of them say they are innocent. The third woman changes her story. Fear of witches grows.

Chapter 4: "Dangerous Times"

_____

_____

Chapter 5: "Hang Them!"

_____

_____

QuickWrite

▶ Why do you think the adults believed the girls at first? Explain your answer using details from the book.

_____

_____

Resource Links
Library Teaching Resources: p. 85
SAM Keyword: Witch Hunt

Use with **Library Teaching Resources,** *page 84.*

Killer Croc
by Elizabeth Carney

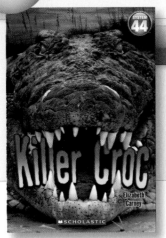

Genre	Pages	Lexile	Audio CD	Reading
Science	24	430	18 min 5 sec	Counts!

Summary

In Burundi, Africa, a giant killer crocodile prowls the shores of the Rusizi River and terrorizes villagers. A man named Patrice Faye names the croc Gustave and spends years trying to capture it. At one point, it seems that Gustave has died. Then in 2006, a giant croc kills ten people near Lake Tanganyika, and the hunt for Gustave resumes.

Phonics Focus

- *r*-controlled vowels *ar*, *er*, *ir*, and *ur*
- Suffixes *–er* and *–or*

See **Master Skills Tracker:** Teacher's Guide, page 548

Skills Tracker

Preteach | Teach/Practice/Apply | Review/Reinforce | Assess

Smart Words

Words are defined on pp. 4–5 of the student book. Page number of first appearance is listed below.

- capture*, p. 15
- dangerous, p. 8
- expose*, p. 15
- fail, p. 16
- reptile*, p. 6
- risk, p. 12
- terror*, p. 12

*Spanish Cognates, **page 14**

Option 1: Decoding

Conference

Ask students to read the Phonics Focus words on the inside back cover of *Killer Croc*. If they struggle with decoding, proceed to individualized instruction.

Individualized Instruction

For words with *r*-controlled vowels *ar*, *er*, *ir*, and *ur*: Have students use the Word Sort decoding routine on **page 21** to sort words by *ar*, *er*, *ir*, and *ur* spellings.

For words with suffixes *-er* and *-or*: Use the Word Parts routine on **page 18** to help students identify and use suffixes.

Option 2: Vocabulary

Conference

Ask students to use some Smart Words from the book in an oral sentence. Review definitions on pages 4–5 as needed. If students demonstrate proficiency, proceed to individualized instruction.

Individualized Instruction

The Smart Word *dangerous* has many possible synonyms and antonyms. Use the **Extending Meaning** vocabulary routine on **page 22** to extend meaning.

Option 3: Fluency

Conference

Ask students to read page 8 of *Killer Croc* aloud. To work on pacing, proceed to individualized instruction.

Individualized Instruction

Use page 8 of *Killer Croc* and the **Read With Expression** fluency routine on **page 29** to have students practice expressive reading.

Comprehension

Use the questions below and the Wrap-Up on **page 87** to check comprehension and promote reader response.

After Chapter 1: *Why is Gustave so dangerous?* (He's huge and kills large animals and people.)

After Chapter 3: *Why doesn't Faye kill Gustave when he finds him?* (He knows that such large crocs are rare. Capturing the croc alive will allow experts to study it.)

End of Book: *What makes Faye think that Gustave might be dead?* (Gustave disappears for a long time.)

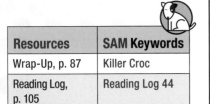

Resources	SAM Keywords
Wrap-Up, p. 87	Killer Croc
Reading Log, p. 105	Reading Log 44

Name _____

Killer Croc

Build Understanding

▶ Fill in the circles with words that tell about Gustave, the killer crocodile. An example is done for you.

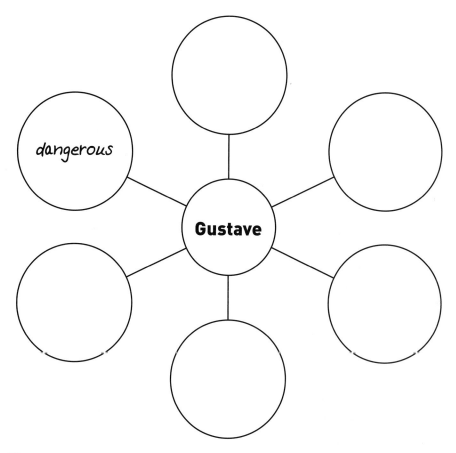

QuickWrite

▶ Why has no one been able to capture Gustave? Write a sentence that tells your opinion. Use at least one word from the circles above to support your answer.

_____

_____

_____

The Promise

by Tracey West

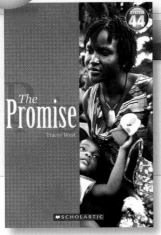

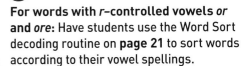

Genre	Pages	Lexile	Audio CD	Reading
Social Studies	24	440	18 min 7 sec	Counts!

Summary

Dr. Julian Atim dedicates her life to helping the people of Uganda. She works where she is needed most to help those with HIV and AIDS. She is also a human rights activist, working to get the people of her country proper health care and to end the country's political conflict with enemy rebels. Dr. Atim inspires others by fighting for what is right.

Phonics Focus

- *r*-controlled vowels *or* and *ore*
- /sh/ spellings *ci* and *ti*

See **Master Skills Tracker:** Teacher's Guide, page 548

Skills Tracker

Preteach | Teach/Practice/Apply | Review/Reinforce | Assess

Smart Words

Words are defined on pp. 4–5 of the student book. Page number of first appearance is listed below.

- **accomplish, p. 18**
- **activist*, p. 17**
- **conflict*, p. 11**
- **continue*, p. 10**
- **dedicate*, p. 7**
- **mission*, p. 7**
- **reform*, p. 16**

*Spanish Cognates, **page 14**

Option 1: Decoding

 Conference

Ask students to read the Phonics Focus words on the inside back cover of *The Promise*. If they struggle with decoding, proceed to individualized instruction.

Individualized Instruction

For words with *r*-controlled vowels *or* and *ore*: Have students use the Word Sort decoding routine on **page 21** to sort words according to their vowel spellings.

For words with /sh/ spellings *ci* and *ti*: Have students use the Word Sort routine to sort words by *ci* and *ti* spellings. Point out that both stand for the /sh/ sound.

Option 2: Vocabulary

 Conference

Ask students to use some Smart Words from the book in an oral sentence. Review definitions on pages 4–5 as needed. If students demonstrate proficiency, proceed to individualized instruction.

Individualized Instruction

Act is the base of the Smart Word *activist* and the words *action*, *active*, *activate*, *activity*, *actor*, and *actress*. Use the **Extending Meaning** vocabulary routine on **page 22** to build student familiarity with morphological word families.

Option 3: Fluency

 Conference

Ask students to read page 9 of *The Promise* aloud. To work on correct phrasing, proceed to individualized instruction.

Individualized Instruction

Use pages 9–11 of *The Promise* and the **Phrasing and Punctuation** fluency routine on **page 26** to have students practice correct phrasing.

Comprehension

Use the questions below and the Wrap-Up on **page 89** to check comprehension and promote reader response.

After Chapter 1: *Where does Dr. Atim work? (in a hospital in Kitgum, Uganda)*

After Chapter 3: *What are two major problems in Uganda? (the fight against AIDS and the rebel army called the LRA)*

End of Book: *What are some things that Dr. Atim dedicates herself to? (She is dedicated to fighting for health and human rights, helping orphans and refugees, and helping women earn more money.)*

Resources	SAM Keywords
Wrap-Up, p. 89	The Promise
Reading Log, p. 105	Reading Log 44

Name _____

The Promise

Build Understanding

▶ As you read, think about the most important ideas or events that happen in each chapter. Then summarize each chapter below in the space provided. An example has been done for you.

Chapter 2: "A Country at War"

Uganda has been fighting a war against the deadly disease of AIDS. It has affected millions of people. Uganda is also fighting the LRA, rebels who want to overthrow the president of Uganda.

Chapter 3: "The Making of a Doctor"

_____

_____

_____

Chapter 4: "An Activist Is Born"

_____

_____

_____

QuickWrite

▶ Dr. Atim is an inspirational person. What aspect of who she is or what she does inspires you the most? Why? Explain your answer using details from the book.

_____

_____

_____

Beauty and the Geek
by Ayana Carter

Genre	Pages	Lexile	Audio CD	Reading
Fiction	24	380	17 min 30 sec	Counts!

Summary

Mia has a crush on Jorge, but Diego, Jorge's geeky brother, has a crush on her. Mia tries to meet Jorge by practicing for band at Diego's house, but is surprised by how much she likes spending time with Diego. Mia sees that Diego is talented and not so geeky after all. Choosing between the brothers is confusing, but eventually Diego wins her heart.

Phonics Focus

- r- controlled vowels -air, -are, and -ear
- Suffixes -er and -est

See **Master Skills Tracker:** Teacher's Guide, page 548

Skills Tracker

Preteach Teach/Practice/Apply Review/Reinforce Assess

Smart Words

Words are defined on pp. 4–5 of the student book. Page number of first appearance is listed below.

- compare*, p. 13
- impress*, p. 9
- interest*, p. 6
- introduce*, p. 8
- jealous, p. 13
- obvious*, p. 9
- plan*, p. 8

*Spanish Cognates, **page 14**

Option 1: Decoding

 Conference

Ask students to read the Phonics Focus words on the inside back cover of *Beauty and the Geek*. If they struggle with decoding, proceed to individualized instruction.

Individualized Instruction

For words with *r*-controlled vowels -air, -are, and -ear: Have students use the Word Sort routine on **page 21** to sort words by -are, -air, and -ear spellings.

For words with suffixes -er and -est: Use the Word Parts decoding routine on **page 18** to help students identify and use suffixes.

Option 2: Vocabulary

 Conference

Ask students to use some Smart Words from the book in an oral sentence. Review definitions on pages 4–5 as needed. If students demonstrate proficiency, proceed to individualized instruction.

 Individualized Instruction

The idiom *got the hang of it* used in the third paragraph of page 17 means "learned how to do something." Build understanding of idioms using the **Idioms** vocabulary routine on **page 25** with this expression as an example.

Option 3: Fluency

Conference

Ask students to read page 12 of *Beauty and the Geek* aloud. To work on expressive reading, proceed to individualized instruction.

Individualized Instruction

Use pages 12–13 of *Beauty and the Geek* and the **Read With Expression** fluency routine on **page 29** to have students practice expressive reading.

Comprehension

Use the questions below and the Wrap-Up on **page 91** to check comprehension and promote reader response.

After Chapter 1: *Who does Mia have a crush on?* (a guy named Jorge, a popular older guy in school)

After Chapter 3: *How does Mia plan to meet Jorge?* (Mia arranges to practice for band with Jorge's brother, Diego.)

End of Book: *What things make Mia realize that she has a crush on Diego?* (She can't stop thinking about Diego while she is out with Jorge. She begins to think Diego is cute. She is thrilled when he asks her to go to the movies.)

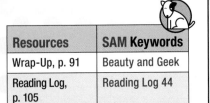

Resources	SAM Keywords
Wrap-Up, p. 91	Beauty and Geek
Reading Log, p. 105	Reading Log 44

Name _____

Beauty and the Geek

Build Understanding

▶ What is Mia thinking? Fill in the thought bubbles below. Write a thought she might have about each topic. The first one is done for you.

Jorge is the cutest guy at school. I really want to meet him.

1. Jorge

2. Her plan to go to Diego's house

3. Diego when he plays the trumpet

4. The party that Jorge takes her to

5. Diego at the end of the story

QuickWrite

▶ Why do you think Mia chooses Diego and not Jorge? Write a sentence that tells your opinion.

_____

_____

_____

Fire! The Triangle Shirtwaist Factory Tragedy

by Tracey West

Genre Social Studies	Pages 24	Lexile 440	Audio CD 18 min 18 sec	Reading Counts!

Summary

In 1911, a fire breaks out in the Triangle Shirtwaist Factory, killing 146 workers. The factory owners are tried for manslaughter but not convicted. A woman named Frances Perkins protests to prevent future tragedies. Thanks to her, laws are passed to make factories safer places to work.

Phonics Focus

- Diphthongs *oi, oy, ou,* and *ow*
- Suffixes *-ful* and *-less*

See **Master Skills Tracker:** Teacher's Guide, page 548

Skills Tracker

Preteach Teach/Practice/Apply Review/Reinforce Assess

Smart Words

Words are defined on pp. 4–5 of the student book. Page number of first appearance is listed below.

- factory*, p. 6
- improve, p. 14
- labor*, p. 14
- prevent*, p. 13
- protest*, p. 14
- strike, p. 14
- tragic*, p. 10

*Spanish Cognates, **page 14**

Option 1: Decoding

 Conference

Ask students to read the Phonics Focus words on the inside back cover of *Fire!* If they struggle with decoding, proceed to individualized instruction.

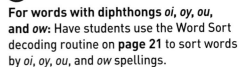 **Individualized Instruction**

For words with diphthongs *oi, oy, ou,* and *ow*: Have students use the Word Sort decoding routine on **page 21** to sort words by *oi, oy, ou,* and *ow* spellings.

For words with suffixes *-ful* and *-less*: Use the Word Parts decoding routine on **page 18** to help students use suffixes.

Option 2: Vocabulary

 Conference

Ask students to use some Smart Words from the book in an oral sentence. Review definitions on pages 4–5 as needed. If students demonstrate proficiency, proceed to individualized instruction.

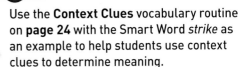 **Individualized Instruction**

Use the **Context Clues** vocabulary routine on **page 24** with the Smart Word *strike* as an example to help students use context clues to determine meaning.

Option 3: Fluency

 Conference

Ask students to read page 9 of *Fire!* aloud. To work on correct phrasing, proceed to individualized instruction.

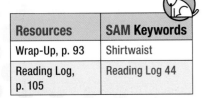 **Individualized Instruction**

Use pages 9–10 of *Fire!* and the **Phrasing and Punctuation** fluency routine on **page 26** to have students practice correct phrasing.

Comprehension

Use the questions below and the Wrap-Up on **page 93** to check comprehension and promote reader response.

After Chapter 1: *Where does the factory fire begin? (in a scrap bin filled with cloth and papers)*

After Chapter 4: *Why does the jury find Blanck and Harris not guilty? (because there is no proof that they knew that the door on the ninth floor was locked)*

End of Book: *Why is Frances Perkins an important woman in the lives of factory workers? (She helps make laws to protect workers.)*

Resources	SAM Keywords
Wrap-Up, p. 93	Shirtwaist
Reading Log, p. 105	Reading Log 44

Name _____

Fire! The Triangle Shirtwaist Factory Tragedy

Build Understanding

▶ Why is the Triangle Shirtwaist Factory an unsafe place to work? Fill in the circles below with reasons. An example has been done for you.

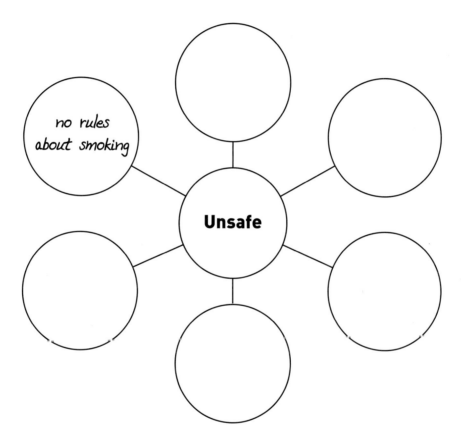

no rules about smoking

Unsafe

QuickWrite

▶ Are the factory owners to blame for the workers' deaths? Tell why or why not. Use one or more details from above.

_____

_____

_____

BOOK 33 — Conference Guide

Hot Jobs
by Richard Camden

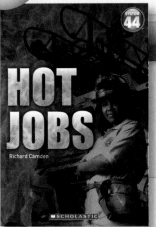

Genre	Pages	Lexile	Audio CD	Reading
Jobs	32	450	24 min 42 sec	Counts!

Summary

This book features five people whose jobs involve working under hot conditions. Scientist Cheryl Gansecki studies volcanoes. Firefighter Keisha Wilson saves lives. Chef Yeny Grusenmeyer works in a hot kitchen. Lifeguard Jon Vipond spends his days in the blazing sun. David Garcia blows molten glass in a superhot furnace.

Phonics Focus

- *oo* and *ew*
- Prefixes *mid-* and *sub-*
- Roots *dict* and *port*

See **Master Skills Tracker:** Teacher's Guide, page 548

Skills Tracker

Preteach | Teach/Practice/Apply | Review/Reinforce | Assess

Smart Words

Words are defined on pp. 4–5 of the student book. Page number of first appearance is listed below.

- career*, p. 16
- equipment*, p. 16
- extreme*, p. 13
- handle, p. 13
- major*, p. 15
- result*, p. 15
- train, p. 6

*Spanish Cognates, **page 15**

Option 1: Decoding

Conference

Ask students to read the Phonics Focus words on the inside back cover of *Hot Jobs.* If they struggle with decoding, proceed to individualized instruction.

Individualized Instruction

For words with *oo* and *ew*: Have students use the Word Sort routine on **page 21** to sort by *oo* and *ew* spellings. Point out that both stand for the long *o* sound.

For words with prefixes *mid-* and *sub*, and roots *dict* and *port*: Use the Word Parts routine on **page 18** to help students identify and use suffixes and roots.

Option 2: Vocabulary

Conference

Ask students to use some Smart Words from the book in an oral sentence. Review definitions on pages 4–5 as needed. If students demonstrate proficiency, proceed to individualized instruction.

Individualized Instruction

The Smart Word *handle* can mean "to deal with or take control" or "the part of an object used to move it." Use the **Multiple-Meaning Words** vocabulary routine on **page 23** with *handle* as an example to help students determine correct meaning.

Option 3: Fluency

Conference

Ask students to read page 8 of *Hot Jobs* aloud. To work on expressive reading, proceed to individualized instruction.

Individualized Instruction

Use pages 8–9 of *Hot Jobs* and the **Read With Expression** fluency routine on **page 29** to have students practice expressive reading.

Comprehension

Use the questions below and the Wrap-Up on **page 95** to check comprehension and promote reader response.

After Chapter 1: *Cheryl has a close call while camping at Kilauea. What happens?* (The wind changes direction, and burning rocks fly toward her.)

After Chapter 4: *What ingredients are in mole?* (chocolate, chiles, garlic, onions, nuts)

End of Book: *What skills does a lifeguard need?* (Lifeguards need to know first aid and be great swimmers.)

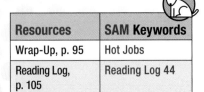

Resources	SAM Keywords
Wrap-Up, p. 95	Hot Jobs
Reading Log, p. 105	Reading Log 44

Name _____

Hot Jobs

Build Understanding

▶ Answer the questions below with details from the book. The first one is done for you.

Chapter 1 Where does Cheryl Gansecki film lava flows? *She films them at the top of a volcano.*	**Chapter 2** How many months of training do firefighters like Keisha Wilson need?	**Chapter 3** Who introduced Yeny Grusenmeyer to cooking?
Chapter 3 What is a sous-chef?	**Chapter 4** What scary rescue does Jon Vipond do at the beach one day?	**Chapter 5** Why does a person need to be strong to blow glass?

QuickWrite

▶ Which job described in this book do you think is the most dangerous? Why? Explain your answer using details from the book.

_____

_____

_____

Everyday Heroes
by Patricia Kean

Genre	Pages	Lexile	Audio CD	Reading
Social Studies	32	440	24 min 48 sec	Counts!

Summary

Read about ordinary people who have risked their lives to help others. Four boys save a girl from an attack. Jose LeGrand stops a runaway car with a little girl inside it. Kelli Groves saves a choking baby. Jeremy Hernandez helps evacuate a school bus stuck on a collapsing bridge. And Wesley Autrey keeps a man from being run over by a train.

Phonics Focus

- *oo* and *u*
- Prefixes *dis-* and *mis-*
- Roots *rupt*, *struct*, and *scrib/script*

See **Master Skills Tracker:** Teacher's Guide, page 548

Skills Tracker

Preteach   Teach/Practice/Apply   Review/Reinforce   Assess

Smart Words

Words are defined on pp. 4–5 of the student book. Page number of first appearance is listed below.
- discovery, p. 10
- distract*, p. 10
- distress, p. 10
- hesitate, p. 12
- instruct*, p. 19
- maneuver*, p. 19
- station*, p. 29

*Spanish Cognates, **page 15**

Option 1: **Decoding**

 Conference

Ask students to read the Phonics Focus words on the inside back cover of *Everyday Heroes*. If they struggle with decoding, proceed to individualized instruction.

 Individualized Instruction

For words *oo* and *u*: Have students use the Word Sort routine on **page 21** to sort words by *oo* and *u* spellings. Review that both spellings can stand for the same sound.

For words with prefixes *dis-* and *mis-*, and roots *rupt*, *struct*, and *scrib/script*: Use the Word Parts decoding routine on **page 18** to help students identify and use prefixes and roots.

Option 2: **Vocabulary**

 Conference

Ask students to use some Smart Words from the book in an oral sentence. Review definitions on pages 4–5 as needed. If students demonstrate proficiency, proceed to individualized instruction.

 Individualized Instruction

Discover is the base of the Smart Word *discovery* and the words *discovered*, *discoveries*, *discovering*, and *discovers*. Use the **Extending Meaning** vocabulary routine on **page 22** to build familiarity with morphological word families.

Option 3: **Fluency**

Conference

Ask students to read page 13 of *Everyday Heroes* aloud. To work on pacing, proceed to individualized instruction.

Individualized Instruction

Use pages 13–15 of *Everyday Heroes* and the **Use Natural, Consistent Pace** fluency routine on **page 27** to have students practice correct pacing.

Comprehension

Use the questions below and the Wrap-Up on **page 97** to check comprehension and promote reader response.

After Chapter 1: *What happens to Samantha while she is riding her bike? (A car hits her, knocking her onto the grass. When she tries to get up, the driver pulls her back down.)*

After Chapter 3: *How do Jose and Maria help save Reiko? (They let Reiko's car smash into theirs, so that her car will come to a stop.)*

End of Book: *What does Wesley do to save Cameron? (Wesley lies on top of Cameron on the train tracks to protect Cameron from being run over.)*

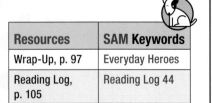

Resources	SAM Keywords
Wrap-Up, p. 97	Everyday Heroes
Reading Log, p. 105	Reading Log 44

Name ______________________________

Everyday Heroes

Build Understanding

▶ Identify the most important things that happen in the chapters listed below. Then summarize each chapter in your own words. One has been done for you.

Chapter 1: "The Fantastic Four"

____

____

____

Chapter 3: "A Baby's Life"

____

____

____

Chapter 5: "Subway Superhero"

A man has a seizure and falls onto the train tracks. Wesley jumps off the platform to save him. A train passes over them but they are unharmed. Wesley is honored for being a hero.

QuickWrite

▶ Which story about everyday heroes inspires you the most? Explain your answer using details from the book.

____

____

____

Resource Links
Library Teaching Resources: p. 97
SAM Keyword: Everyday Heroes

Use with **Library Teaching Resources,** *page 96.*

Arabian Nights

A Graphic Classic Based on Traditional Stories

by **Terry West**

	Genre	Pages	Lexile	Audio CD	Reading
	Graphic Classic	32	340	23 min 1 sec	Counts!

Summary

In this graphic classic retelling, a sultan's wife and brother plot against him. The Sultan kills his wife by mistake and banishes his brother. Afraid of being betrayed again, the Sultan vows to kill his new wife on their wedding day. Scheherazade, his new wife, soothes the Sultan and keeps herself alive by telling a new story every night.

Phonics Focus

- *a, au,* and *aw*
- Suffixes *-sion* and *-tion*
- Root *graph*

See **Master Skills Tracker:**
Teacher's Guide, page 548

Skills Tracker

Preteach   Teach/Practice/Apply   Review/Reinforce   Assess

Smart Words

Words are defined on pp. 4–5 of the student book. Page number of first appearance is listed below.

- advisor, p. 10
- betray, p. 7
- greedy, p. 7
- majesty*, p. 10
- nightmare, p. 9
- supply, p. 7
- treasure, p. 14

*Spanish Cognates, **page 15**

Option 1: **Decoding**

 Conference

Ask students to read the Phonics Focus words on the inside back cover of *Arabian Nights*. If they struggle with decoding, proceed to individualized instruction.

 Individualized Instruction

For words with a, au, and aw : Have students use the Word Sort decoding routine on **page 21** to sort words by *a, au,* and *aw* spellings.

For words with suffixes –sion and –tion, and root graph: Use the Word Parts routine on **page 18** to help students identify and use suffixes and roots.

Option 2: **Vocabulary**

 Conference

Ask students to use some Smart Words listed on the inside back cover of *Arabian Nights* in an oral sentence. Review definitions on pages 4–5 as needed. If students demonstrate proficiency, proceed to individualized instruction.

 Individualized Instruction

Advice is the base of the Smart Word *advisor* and the words *advised, advises, advisors, advising, advisory, advisable,* and *unadvisable.* Use the **Extending Meaning** vocabulary routine on **page 22** to build student familiarity with morphological word families.

Option 3: **Fluency**

 Conference

Ask students to read page 10 of *Arabian Nights* aloud. To work on expressive reading, proceed to individualized instruction.

 Individualized Instruction

Use pages 10–12 of *Arabian Nights* and the **Read With Expression** fluency routine on **page 29** to have students practice expressive reading.

Comprehension

Use the questions below and the Wrap-Up on **page 99** to check comprehension and promote reader response.

After Page 9: *Why must the Sultan take another wife? (The law says he must remarry, or the kingdom will go to his brother.)*

After Page 19: *In the story of Ali Baba, what happens to Kasim? (Kasim forgets the password and is trapped in the cave. When the thieves return, they kill him.)*

End of Book: *How do Scheherazade's tales help the Sultan? (They ease his mind so that he can fall asleep. The tale of Aladdin gives him hope that he and his wife can be happy.)*

Resources	SAM Keywords
Wrap-Up, p. 99	Arabian Nights
Reading Log, p. 105	Reading Log 44

Wrap-Up

Book 35

Name ____________________

Arabian Nights

Build Understanding

▶ Details are bits of information. Fill in the chart below with at least two details about each of the characters. One has been done for you.

Character	Details
The Sultan	▪ *Was betrayed by his wife and brother* ▪ *Is scared that any new wife will also betray him*
Scheherazade	
Ali Baba	
Kasim	
Morgiana	
Aladdin	

QuickWrite

▶ Which character from these stories is the most creative? Why do you think so? Write at least two sentences.

____

____

____

Resource Links
Library Teaching Resources: p. 99
SAM Keyword: Arabian Nights

Use with **Library Teaching Resources,** *page 98.*

BOOK **36** Conference Guide

Lost! Mysteries of the Bermuda Triangle by Emily Costello

Genre	Pages	Lexile	Audio CD	Reading
Science	32	440	24 min 27 sec	Counts

Summary

Many ships, planes, and people have vanished without a trace in the Bermuda Triangle. Some people think the area is cursed, but others propose more reasonable explanations. Pirates, the dangerous Sargasso Sea, giant squid, blue holes, sandbars, malfunctioning compasses, and inexperienced pilots are all plausible explanations.

Phonics Focus

- Prefix *tri-*
- Suffixes *-able* and *-ible*
- Roots *phon*, *scope*, *tele*, and *vis/vid*

See **Master Skills Tracker:** Teacher's Guide, page 548

Skills Tracker

Preteach Teach/Practice/Apply Review/Reinforce Assess

Smart Words

Words are defined on pp. 4–5 of the student book. Page number of first appearance is listed below.

- **current*, p. 17**
- **disappear*, p. 6**
- **panic*, p. 14**
- **surrounded, p. 10**
- **unpredictable*, p. 8**
- **violent*, p. 16**
- **visible*, p. 6**

*Spanish Cognates, **page 15**

Option 1: Decoding

 Conference

Ask students to read the Phonics Focus words on the inside back cover of *Lost!* If they struggle with decoding, proceed to individualized instruction.

 Individualized Instruction

For words with prefix *tri-*, suffixes *-able* and *-ible*, and roots *phon*, *scope*, *tele*, and *vis/vid*: Use the Word Parts decoding routine on **page 18** to help students identify and use prefixes, suffixes, and roots.

Option 2: Vocabulary

 Conference

Ask students to use some Smart Words from the book in an oral sentence. Review definitions on pages 4–5 as needed. If students demonstrate proficiency, proceed to individualized instruction.

 Individualized Instruction

Use the **Context Clues** vocabulary routine on **page 24** with the Smart Word *current* as an example to help students use context clues to determine meaning.

Option 3: Fluency

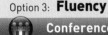 **Conference**

Ask students to read page 19 of *Lost!* aloud. To practice expressive reading, proceed to individualized instruction.

 Individualized Instruction

Use pages 19–20 of *Lost!* and the **Read With Expression** fluency routine on **page 29** to have students practice reading in a varied, expressive tone.

Comprehension

Use the questions below and the Wrap-Up on **page 101** to check comprehension and promote reader response.

After Chapter 2: *Why is the Sargasso Sea dangerous? (It's calm, windless, and filled with seaweed, so ships can get stuck.)*

After Chapter 4: *What could explain why planes get lost in the Bermuda Triangle? (Sometimes compasses don't work in the Triangle. Planes can also get caught in a storm.)*

End of Book: *What are rogue waves and why are they so scary? (Rogue waves are monster waves. They are unpredictable and can form anytime, even in good weather.)*

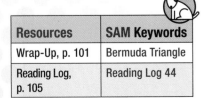

Resources	SAM Keywords
Wrap-Up, p. 101	Bermuda Triangle
Reading Log, p. 105	Reading Log 44

Name _____

Lost! Mysteries of the Bermuda Triangle

Build Understanding

▶ There are many explanations for the disappearances in the Bermuda Triangle. Fill in each circle below with an explanation. An example is done for you.

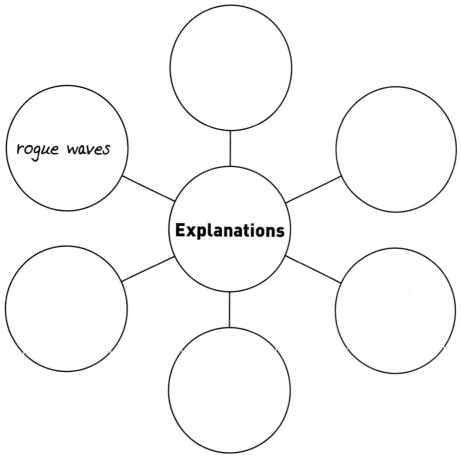

rogue waves

Explanations

QuickWrite

▶ Would you rather travel through the Bermuda Triangle in a plane or a ship? Tell your opinion. Use details from the book to support your answer.

_____

_____

_____

Name ______________________________

Word Sort

▶ Use this page to sort words by sound or spelling. Write the sounds or spellings you will use in the top row of the chart below. Then, fill in each column with words that have that sound or spelling.

SOUND OR SPELLING ________	**SOUND OR SPELLING** ________	**SOUND OR SPELLING** ________	**SOUND OR SPELLING** ________

Resource Links
Library Teaching Resources: p. 102
SAM Keyword: Word Sort 44

Name _____

Vocabulary Builder

▶ Use the chart below to list new words you come across in your reading. For each word, write a definition and a short sentence that uses the word.

Book Title _____

NEW WORD	DEFINITION	MY SENTENCE

Fluency Checklist

▶ Use this checklist to keep a record of progress. Write the date and the reader's name. Then, make checkmarks to show what improved. Add helpful comments if you like.

Date _____

Name _____

Accuracy

___ Skipped words

___ Read every word

___ Self-corrected

Speed

___ Too slow

___ Just right

___ Too fast

Expression

___ Paid attention to end punctuation

___ Paused at commas and used phrasing

___ Read with expression

Name _____

Reading Log

▶ Use this page to record your daily reading.

DATE	TITLE	STARTING PAGE	ENDING PAGE	NOTES

Answer Key

The following are answers from the Build Understanding portions of the Wrap-Ups.

Book 1: *Bugs That Kill*, **p. 31**
Answers may vary. Possible answers include:
Praying Mantis: This bug has bug eyes and a small head. It kills other bugs.
Killer Bee: They can kill big animals. They fly in a big mob.
Scorpion: Its tail has poison. It mostly kills bugs.
Fire Ant: This bug stings. The sting feels like fire!

Book 2: *Messy Jobs*, **p. 33**
Answers may vary. Possible answers include:
Ship Painter: The old paint and the new paint get all over me!
Podiatrist: Cutting people's nails and taking off bumps can be messy!
Motocross Racer: Mud flies onto my bike and my clothes!

Book 3: *Yes!*, **p. 35**
Chantal Petitclerc: Chantal shouts, "Yes!" because she finishes first in the race.
Dwight Howard: Dwight shouts, "Yes!" because he makes the basket.
Pete Carroll: Pete shouts, "Yes!" because his team has won.

Book 4: *Fast!*, **p. 37**
Answers may vary. Possible answers include:
They can run 71 miles per hour. Their claws grip the ground. They get hot when they run. They have to rest after running. They run faster than speed limits!

Book 5: *These Are Not Poems*, **p. 39**
Answers may vary. Possible answers include:
2. I know who I am. Others don't know the real me.
3. People love to guess if I like the new boy.
4. Momma taught me how to cook.
5. Real-life heroes have to work hard.

Book 6: *Wonders of the World*, **p. 41**
Answers may vary. Possible answers include:
Pyramids of Giza: The pyramids are made of stone blocks. They are really old. The kings of Egypt are buried inside the pyramids.
Great Wall of China: The Great Wall is so long that it can be seen from space. The wall was built to protect China.
Statue of Liberty: The Statue of Liberty was a gift from France. It was put up in 1886. It is in New York Harbor.

Book 7: *What's New? A History of Invention*, **p. 43**
Second: Thomas Edison shows movies.
Next: An actress wears false eyelashes.
Then: A man invents a baseball bat.
Last: Doctors test the first fake heart.

Book 8: *Yo, Yolanda! Advice About Friends*, **p. 45**
2. Yolanda says the boy should ask for his cash back and not lend his friend any more money.
3. Yolanda says the girl should tell her friend how she feels. If the friend is really a friend, she'll spend time with her too.
4. Yolanda says the shy girl should try joining teams and clubs to meet new people.
5. Yolanda says that the girl should give her friend's ring back.

Book 9: *Is This Art?*, **p. 47**
Answers may vary. Possible answers include:
metal, ordinary stuff, electronic parts, glass, ice

Book 10: *DJ Mystery*, **p. 49**
Answers may vary. Possible answers include:
Second: Jen makes fun of Keith at lunchtime.
Third: Trina and Keith talk about going to the party.
Fourth: Seth stops Keith at the door.
Next: Jen asks Keith to dance with her.
Last: Keith dances with Trina.

Book 11: *Survival Guide: How to Keep Your Job*, **p. 51**
Answers may vary. Possible answers include:
1. Be responsible. Do not call in sick if you are not.
3. Stay cool. Maybe you need to do better. Try asking your boss not to yell. If nothing works, then you may need a new job.
4. Be polite and smile. Tell your boss how great you are. List reasons why you should get a raise.

Book 12: *Fashion Flashback*, **p. 53**
Answers may vary. Possible answers include:
light and loose dresses, shoulder pads, preppy shirts, stretched-out shirts, jeans with holes

Book 13: *Button Your Lip and Other Idioms*, **p. 55**
2. Do not talk
3. Do not tell a secret
4. To be right
5. Slow down
6. Think about a problem
7. Say the wrong thing at the wrong time
8. Hurry

Book 14: *African Journey*, **p. 57**
Answers may vary. Possible answers include:
Going on Safari: It is very dry here. Many animals migrate in the Serengeti National Park.
Animal Buddies: Zebras help each other watch for dangerous lions. Birds help keep elephants' skin clean by eating bugs.
On the Hunt: Cheetahs can run up to 70 miles per hour. A group of lions is called a pride.
Visiting the Maasai: The Maasai raise cattle for milk and meat. The Maasai build their houses in a circle.

Book 15: *Ripped From the Headlines*, **p. 59**
Answers may vary. Possible answers include:
"Stranger Danger!": Palmira Gonzalez-Jiminez is in gym class when a man grabs her. Her friends rescue her from the man.
"Falling Baby!": Felix Vasquez is outside a burning building. A mother and her baby are trapped inside. The mother tosses the baby to Felix. Felix safely catches the baby.
"Trapped!": Aron Ralston is hiking when a big rock rolls onto his arm and traps him. After five days he cuts off his arm and hikes to a hospital for help.

Book 16: *The Princess Brat*, **p. 61**
Answers may vary. Possible answers include:
spoiled, lazy, annoyed, impatient, famous

Book 17: *Cool Jobs in Basketball*, **p. 63**
Answers may vary. Possible answers include:
Tony: I write about pro basketball for a Web site. I get to travel to basketball games and talk to athletes. I am living my dream!
Keith: I'm a trainer for professional basketball teams. I teach exercises to hurt athletes to help them get better.

Book 18: *When Lisa Met Billy*, **p. 65**
2. Lisa helps Billy rehearse.
3. Lisa fills in for Angie.

Book 19: *Crash!*, p. 67
Answers may vary. Possible answers include:

Chapter 1: An asteroid is a big rock found in space. If an asteroid hits Earth it will cause a lot of damage. Scientists follow the paths of asteroids so we know if one may hit Earth.

Chapter 3: Asteroids are left over from when planets formed billions of years ago. Experts study them to learn about what Earth was like back then. Telescopes help experts see more asteroids.

Book 20: *Back From the Grave!*, p. 69
Chapter 2: She looks so alive!

Chapter 3: He sees Juliet in a bloody white dress.

Chapter 4: He cuts off her fingers to steal her rings.

Book 21: *El Tiburón*, p. 71
Second: Sergio dreams that the ocean speaks to him.

Next: Sergio hires a swimming coach.

Then: Sergio swims the Strait of Gibraltar.

Last: Sergio swims for 24 hours in Marcos's honor.

Book 22: *Medical Miracle*, p. 73
2. They appear on the news to ask the people of Peru for help.

3. The doctor has to stretch her skin.

4. Milagros will need to have more surgeries.

Book 23: *Disaster!*, p. 75
Answers may vary. Possible answers include:

Kaci: The tornado was really scary. It knocked down trees and damaged a lot of homes. I was scared for my family.

Fitri: We lost everything we owned in the tsunami. So many people lost loved ones also. I'm grateful that my family survived.

Troy: Hurricane Katrina was one of the worst things that I've been through. We lost many things in the hurricane. I'm glad to be back in New Orleans now, though.

Book 24: *The Sweater Thief*, p. 77
Answers may vary. Possible answers include:

Tracey: I'm glad I didn't let you get away with stealing. You were never really my friend.

Kayla: I can't believe you told on me. I'm going to tell everyone at school to ignore you.

Book 25: *Left to Die*, p. 79
2. Simon cuts the rope.

3. Joe lowers himself down.

4. Joe crawls for four days.

Book 26: *Samurai Fighters*, p. 81
Answers may vary. Possible answers include:
carry two swords, wear body armor, masks, helmets, long robes, hair long in the back

Book 27: *Ant Attack!*, p. 83
Second: The workers build two ditches.

Third: Rodriguez ignites the gas to make a wall of fire.

Fourth: Rodriguez runs to open up the dam.

Last: Workers pick the ants off Rodriguez and carry him to the barn roof.

Book 28: *Witch Hunt*, p. 85
Answers may vary. Possible answers include:

Chapter 1: Betty and Abigail are acting strangely. A doctor says a witch has taken over their bodies.

Chapter 2: The girls say that three women in town are witches. They pick women that aren't popular in town. People in Salem Village are scared.

Chapter 4: More people are named as witches. The Proctors are named. They also say Mary is a witch.

Chapter 5: People in Salem Village keep being arrested as witches. Some people are hanged. The governor stops the witch trials after his wife is named as a witch.

Book 29: *Killer Croc*, p. 87
Answers may vary. Possible answers include:
reptile, at least 20 feet long, weighs about 2,000 pounds, lives in Burundi, hasn't been caught

Book 30: *The Promise*, p. 89
Answers may vary. Possible answers include:

Chapter 3: Julian's parents become sick from AIDS. Her mother is not able to afford drugs that would help. Julian decides to become a doctor so that she can help others.

Chapter 4: Julian wants the government of Uganda to change the health-care policies. She wants them to be fair to all people.

Book 31: *Beauty and the Geek*, p. 91
Answers may vary. Possible answers include:

2. I will pretend to be friends with Diego to get near Jorge.

3. Diego is a great trumpet player.

4. The party isn't that fun.

5. I like Diego now.

Book 32: *Fire! The Triangle Shirtwaist Tragedy*, p. 93
Answers may vary. Possible answers include:
don't get paid much, long hours, owners lock the doors, children work there, the fire escape is old

Book 33: *Hot Jobs*, p. 95
Answers may vary. Possible answers include:

Chapter 2: Firefighters train for four months.

Chapter 3: She used to watch her mother cook.

Chapter 3: A sous-chef is second in command in the kitchen.

Chapter 4: He had to rescue 6 people at once.

Chapter 5: The person needs to be strong to handle the heavy equipment.

Book 34: *Everyday Heroes*, p. 97
Answers may vary. Possible answers include:

Chapter 1: A man tries to hurt a teenage girl, but boys from her town are able to help her.

Chapter 3: Kelli Groves is able to save a baby who is not breathing by remembering how to do the Heimlich maneuver she learned in school.

Book 35: *Arabian Nights*, p. 99
Answers may vary. Possible answers include:

Scheherazade: Volunteers to marry the Sultan; tells the Sultan stories every night

Ali Baba: Finds treasure in a cave; offers to share the treasure with his brother

Kasim: Wants the treasure to himself; killed by the forty thieves

Morgiana: Is Ali Baba's servant; pours boiling oil into all of the jars

Aladdin: Gets the lamp from the cave; wants to marry the princess

Book 36: *Lost! Mysteries of the Bermuda Triangle*, p. 101
Answers may vary. Possible answers include:
blue holes, ocean trenches, compasses sometimes don't work, waterspouts, sandbars

Index

Book Cover Credits

BUGS THAT KILL by Peggy Bresnick Kendler. Copyright © 2009 by Scholastic Inc. Published by Scholastic Inc. Cover: Jerome Wexler/ Photo Researchers, Inc.

MESSY JOBS by Alan Takamura. Copyright © 2009 by Scholastic Inc. Published by Scholastic Inc. Cover: Steve Giberson/ Transworld.

YES! GREAT MOMENTS IN SPORTS by Ellen Lebrecque. Copyright © 2009 by Scholastic Inc. Published by Scholastic Inc. Cover: Brian Bahr/Getty Images.

FAST! THE WORLD'S FASTEST COUCH AND OTHER FAST THINGS by Juliette Caggiano. Copyright © 2009 by Scholastic Inc. Published by Scholastic Inc. Cover: Raymonds Press Agency.

THESE ARE NOT POEMS (AND OTHER POEMS) by Tina Posner, illustrated by Carmen Segovia. Copyright © 2009 by Scholastic Inc. Published by Scholastic Inc.

WONDERS OF THE WORLD by Joshua Davis. Copyright © 2009 by Scholastic Inc. Published by Scholastic Inc. Cover: (bl) Brian A. Vikander/Mira.com/drr.net, (tl) Joseph Feltham/iStockphoto, (tr) David Sutherland/ drr.net, (br) Wesley Hitt/Getty Images, (c) NASA.

WHAT'S NEW? A HISTORY OF INVENTION by Peter Gutiérrez. Copyright © 2009 by Scholastic Inc. Published by Scholastic Inc. Cover: (tl) Bettmann/Corbis, (tc) Karovka/ Shutterstock, (tr) Smithsonian Institution/ Corbis, (bl) Hot Ideas/Index Open, (bc) Photodisc via SODA, (br) Steve Marcus/ Reuters.

YO, YOLANDA! ADVICE ABOUT FRIENDS by Kim Feltes and Elsa Reyes, illustrated by Grace Chen. Illustrations copyright © 2009 by Grace Chen. Published by Scholastic Inc.

IS THIS ART? by Grace Nguyen. Copyright © 2009 by Scholastic Inc. Published by Scholastic Inc. Cover: (t) Luis Carlos Torres/ iStockphoto, (b) Ethan Myerson/iStockphoto.

DJ MYSTERY by Michael Leviton, illustrated by Shingo Shimizu. Copyright © 2009 by Scholastic Inc. Published by Scholastic Inc.

SURVIVAL GUIDE: HOW TO KEEP YOUR JOB by Chris Kensler, illustrated by Matt Dorfman. Copyright © 2009 by Scholastic Inc. Published by Scholastic Inc.

FASHION FLASHBACK by Richard Camden. Copyright © 2009 by Scholastic Inc. Published by Scholastic Inc. Cover: (l) Reuters/Corbis, (c) Ron Stewart/SuperStock, (r) Hulton Archive/ Getty Images.

BUTTON YOUR LIP AND OTHER IDIOMS by Polly Downes, illustrated by Debbie Palen. Illustrations copyright © 2009 by Debbie Palen. Published by Scholastic Inc.

AFRICAN JOURNEY by Leslie Bakke and Susan O'Connor. Copyright © 2009 by Scholastic Inc. Published by Scholastic Inc. Cover: Leslie Bakke, (background) Felix Möcke/iStockphoto.

RIPPED FROM THE HEADLINES by Peter Gutiérrez. Copyright © 2009 by Scholastic Inc. Published by Scholastic Inc. Cover: Steve Robertson/Zuma Press, (background) Stephen Firmender.

THE PRINCESS BRAT by Jennifer Johnson, illustrated by Liza Corbett. Illustrations copyright © 2006 by Liza Corbett. Published by Scholastic Inc.

COOL JOBS IN BASKETBALL by Peter Gutiérrez. Copyright © 2009 by NBA Properties, Inc. Published by Scholastic Inc. Cover: Adam Borkowski/Shutterstock.

WHEN LISA MET BILLY by Jorge Ramaldo, illustrated by Ben Shannon. Copyright © 2009 by Scholastic Inc. Published by Scholastic Inc.

CRASH! by Steph Smith. Copyright © 2009 by Scholastic Inc. Published by Scholastic Inc. Cover: Denis Scott/Corbis.

BACK FROM THE GRAVE! based on the story "The Mannerism" by Guy de Maupassant, by Michael Leviton, illustrated by Jim Nelson. Illustrations copyright © 2004 by Jim Nelson. Published by Scholastic Inc.

EL TIBURÓN "THE SHARK" by Patrick Daley. Copyright © 2009 by Scholastic Inc. Published by Scholastic Inc. Cover: Don Bartletti/Los Angeles Times.

MEDICAL MIRACLE by Allison Langley. Copyright © 2009 by Scholastic Inc. Published by Scholastic Inc. Cover: Enrique Castro-Mendivil/Reuters, (background) Matthew Borkoski/Index Stock Imagery.

DISASTER! by Sean Price. Copyright © 2009 by Scholastic Inc. Published by Scholastic Inc. Cover: Dave Martin/AP Images.

THE SWEATER THIEF by Ayana Carter, illustrated by Daniel Chen. Illustrations copyright © 2009 Daniel Chen. Published by Scholastic Inc.

LEFT TO DIE by Nancy Honovich. Copyright © 2009 by Scholastic Inc. Published by Scholastic Inc. Cover: ImageDJ/Index Open, (inset) IFC Films/courtesy Everett Collection.

SAMURAI FIGHTERS by Mel Friedman, illustrated by Red Hansen. Illustrations copyright © 2003 by Red Hansen. Published by Scholastic Inc.

ANT ATTACK! based on Carl Stephenson's short story "Leiningen Versus the Ants," by Michael Leviton, illustrated by Craig Phillips. Illustrations copyright © 2004 by Craig Phillips. Published by Scholastic Inc.

WITCH HUNT by Carol Domblewski, illustrated by Sally Wern Comport. Illustrations copyright © 2003 by Sally Wern Comport. Published by Scholastic Inc.

KILLER CROC by Elizabeth Carney. Copyright © 2009 by Scholastic Inc. Published by Scholastic Inc. Cover: Frans Lanting/Minden Pictures.

THE PROMISE: A UGANDAN DOCTOR'S MISSION by Tracey West. Copyright © 2009 by Scholastic Inc. Published by Scholastic Inc. Cover: Evelyn Hockstein/Polaris.

BEAUTY AND THE GEEK by Ayana Carter, illustrated by Luisa Montalto. Copyright © 2009 by Scholastic Inc. Published by Scholastic Inc.

FIRE! THE TRIANGLE SHIRTWAIST FACTORY TRAGEDY by Tracey West. Copyright © 2009 by Scholastic Inc. Published by Scholastic Inc. Cover: Bettmann/Corbis, (tl) Library of Congress, (rc) Kheel Center for Labor Management Documentation Archives, Cornell University/ILR.

HOT JOBS by Richard Camden. Copyright © 2009 by Scholastic Inc. Published by Scholastic Inc. Cover: Kelly LaDuke.

EVERYDAY HEROES by Patricia Kean. Copyright © 2009 by Scholastic Inc. Published by Scholastic Inc. Cover (tl) Lori Adamski-Peek, (tr) Dynamic Graphics/Jupiter Images, (bl) Dan Henry/AP Images, (br) Ray Tammara/ Getty Images.

ARABIAN NIGHTS based on traditional stories, by Terry M. West, illustrated by Michael Lilly. Copyright © 2009, 2001 by Scholastic Inc. Published by Scholastic Inc.

LOST! MYSTERIES OF THE BERMUDA TRIANGLE by Emily Costello. Copyright © 2009 by Scholastic Inc. Published by Scholastic Inc.